"*Experiments in Honesty* is a fresh take on Christian spirituality and a fantastic read. Unpacking traditional Scripture in a frank, it's-okay-to-question-everything narrative, Steve Daugherty draws you into his life and faith, quietly daring you to lift the veil and take another look at your own. Each chapter is a little bit like exposure therapy to the truth, pushing you to be more honest with yourself and your faith. If you read nothing else but the title, you have already begun your journey in faith and your own experiment with honesty. This is a must read!"

—Anne Kubitsky
Founder & CEO of The Look for the Good Project
and author of *What Makes You Grateful?*

"Steve Daugherty writes as a practical mystic, inviting readers to discover more in everyday moments and those stories we've read numerous times in the Bible. He encourages self-contemplation through his humor and insightful perspective of life. You'll see with fresh eyes as you continually wonder how you've never had these thoughts before. Grab a coffee to drink deeply as you read through *Experiments in Honesty*. You'll notice yourself exploring profoundly into your journey with Jesus at the same time."

—Jeremy Jernigan
Lead pastor of Abundant Life Church
and author of *Redeeming Pleasure*

EXPERIMENTS
IN
HONESTY

EXPERIMENTS IN HONESTY

MEDITATIONS ON LOVE, FEAR AND THE HONEST TO GOD NAKED TRUTH

STEVE DAUGHERTY

WORTHY®
PUBLISHING

Published by Worthy Books, an imprint of Worthy Publishing Group, a division of Worthy Media, Inc., One Franklin Park, 6100 Tower Circle, Suite 210, Franklin, TN 37067.

WORTHY is a registered trademark of Worthy Media, Inc.

HELPING PEOPLE EXPERIENCE THE HEART OF GOD

eBook available wherever digital books are sold.

Library of Congress Cataloging-in-Publication Data

Names: Daugherty, Steve, author.
Title: Experiments in honesty : meditations on love, fear, and the honest to
  God naked truth / Steve Daugherty.
Description: Franklin, TN : Worthy Publishing, 2017. | Includes
  bibliographical references.
Identifiers: LCCN 2017054501 | ISBN 9781683971351 (tradepaper)
Subjects: LCSH: God (Christianity)--Worship and love. | Fear of
  God--Christianity. | God (Christianity)--Love.
Classification: LCC BV4817 .D38 2017 | DDC 231.7--dc23
LC record available at https://lccn.loc.gov/2017054501

For foreign and subsidiary rights, contact rights@worthypublishing.com.

Published in association with The Christopher Ferebee Agency, www.christopherferebee.com.

ISBN: 978-1-68397-135-1

Cover Design: Kent Jensen | Knail
Cover Image: Steve Daugherty
Interior Design and Typesetting: Bart Dawson

Printed in the United States of America
18 19 20 21 22 23 DPI 8 7 6 5 4 3 2 1

CONTENTS

Truth and Lie went for a swim. After a while, Lie got out of the water, put on Truth's clothes, and ran into a nearby town. Unwilling to wear Lie's clothes, Truth also got out of the water and chased Lie naked. As Truth reached the town limits, he was turned away for being naked. Lie, of course, was let right in, looking enough like Truth to go unchallenged.

PART ONE

Naked *or* Afraid

'Twas grace that taught my heart to fear,
and grace my fears relieved . . .

John Newton, "Amazing Grace"

Quintessential Love purges fear.

1 John 4:18, my rendering

1

Too afraid of God to not be afraid of God

HIP-DEEP IN SEAWATER and dragging their boats ashore with exhausted hands, Peter—who at this point in the story still went by Simon—as well as the other fishermen heard someone speaking.

A group of a dozen or so was huddled together, walking along the beach, listening to a man talk. A predawn prayer group, by the looks of it. The tired anglers pretended not to notice them, but they did. *Must be nice to have that kind of time.* Peter noticed the group moving in their direction; a rabbi flanked by men and women eating up his words like fish used to gobble bait in these waters before the empire had fished it nearly empty.

The group continued moving until it was on top of Peter and his crew, and then it stopped. The rabbi kept walking, away from the group, sloshing out to Peter's boat and legging over the side while the crowd watched. The rabbi just got in and sat down.

The fishermen's lined foreheads said it all: *With all due respect, what's this guy think he's doing?*

The rabbi asked to put out a bit, seemingly oblivious to the crew's hollow, tired hearts. They'd been out all night with no fish tales to tell. The crowd stared at Peter, pressuring him with their eyes. With a sigh, Peter motioned to a few of the others to push back out in the water. Rabbis deserved honor, yes. *But he better not press his luck after a night like we've just had.*

The teacher spoke from the boat toward the shore, and it took no time at all for Peter and the others to recognize a simple power in his teaching. Not counterfeit power, one pretended with high volume and ultimatums. The markets were full of mouthy two-bit prophets like that, their fists in the air and their tails on fire. This rabbi was different. It was clear this one had gone out on the water for amplification, because it was too easy to confuse shouting for strength.

The man's words were rich, and yet they weren't all that exotic. He spoke persuasively, but not as the salesmen and the oracles did. It was an artwork of traditional-sounding speech braided with an awareness of coming realities that seemed ready to break in at any moment. Like a familiar door hinged to the jamb of a great palace. The men wondered among themselves, *We've heard this before, haven't we? Or have we?*

Then the rabbi asked to go fishing.

"Sir, respectfully, we're really tired. We've fished all night and pulled nothing but water into this boat." The rabbi nodded but seemed to not understand that Peter was objecting. Someone in the crowd cleared her throat as wives and mothers do to force consent. "All right. Since this is what you want"—Peter directed a mock bow toward the rabbi—"it looks like that's what we're doing."

Peter and his crew pushed their boat out into the waters. It took several minutes to get out far enough to reasonably expect a catch. The four men threw the net out halfheartedly, the weights on the corners splashing into the chop, their aching hands and legs protesting the beginning of a double shift. Each of the men leaned over, watching the net sink. Andrew and John loosely palmed one of the pull ropes as it unwound into the water. James and Peter managed the other. The net disappeared.

After a few moments Peter nodded to the others. *That's enough.* They began to lift the net hand over hand while the rabbi peered over the side, naive and expectant.

Then Andrew was shrieking. "Whoa, whoa, whoa!" The men's arms pulled taut and the boat listed. The rabbi stepped back to the high side of the boat, laughing.

Peter looked to the others on shore. "Come throw another net! C'mon!" he yelled, tugging and frantic. "Hurry!" The rope popped and groaned in the men's hands as they shouted orders at one another. A convulsion of fish broke the surface in a flash of tails and scales gleaming in the sun. Soon the second boat was a few yards away, its net cast close. They immediately found themselves in the same tussle. Those on shore laughed and clapped, more amused than awestruck at the crews' frenzy of yelps and ropes and tangled legs.

Peter's boat was full. The second boat was as well. Writhing tilapia, binys, and sardines where only bare floor planks had been before. Both vessels squatted blessedly low in the water. Amazement replaced exhaustion. It was a miracle by anyone's standard. God had poured out tangible, scaly goodness on Peter and his crew and their families.

No doubt Peter had prayed during that long night. Frankly, it's impossible to believe there hadn't been one clenched-jaw petition for at least breakfast to swim into the nets. Whatever Peter said, I'm persuaded the catch of fish was an unambiguous answer to an unrecorded prayer.

Anyone would've said God had answered this prayer by way of this mysterious man standing in the boat with Peter, knee-deep in fish. This moment had been pure blessing. A gift. An act of Love.

So how did Simon Peter react when this Rabbi Jesus miraculously filled two boats with fish? Pay attention, because Peter does a lot of reacting in the Bible . . .

One time Jesus started glowing right in front of Peter. Moses and Elijah appeared with Jesus on a mountain. They were maybe also glowing. It's hard to say how Peter knew this was Moses and Elijah before the advent of photography, but Peter seemed sure enough to start talking of his religious intentions. Religious men have often been the first to speak with certainty of mysterious things. And so Peter was suddenly speaking: "Jesus, I know . . . I'll make some tents, one for each of you!" It was a sincere offer. It was the most meaningful gesture Peter could imagine in that moment. However, Peter was told to shut up and listen, more or less, when God's voice broke through the clouds and commanded everyone to listen to Jesus.

Another time Peter, along with the other disciples, sent children away so they wouldn't bother Jesus. "Seen and not heard," as the saying goes. Jesus in turn put a child on his lap and explained to the crowd, and to Peter, that God highly values what society ranks low.

Another time Peter was involved in sending hungry people away so they could go feed themselves. "God helps those who help themselves" goes another adage. Jesus contradicted this as well with a mass feeding of fish and chips, along with a reminder that spiritual and physical needs are two sides of the same coin.

Another time Peter told Jesus that he was wrong concerning his own crucifixion. The biblical text actually says Peter rebuked Jesus for saying he'd soon suffer a criminal's demise. True messiahs, after all, don't get crucified. Everyone knew this. Jesus responded by calling his friend Peter "Satan" and telling him to stay out of his way.

Another time, when Jesus was being arrested, Peter lunged forward with a sword. To Peter it seemed reasonable that true messiahs needed to be physically defended by armed apprentices. Peter was going for the officer's head but only connected with his ear. Jesus told Peter he was perpetuating the wrong movement and the wrong religion and commanded that Peter stow his weapon—to use it for no more than filleting fish—and then he healed Peter's victim. Remarkable, I think, that Jesus was having to heal the victims of his church so early on.

Another time Peter puffed out his chest and said, "I will never leave your side, Master." Jesus winced and told Peter that he would not only do exactly that, but would do so three times before the rooster announced breakfast.

Another time Jesus asked Peter who he thought Jesus was. "The Christ, the Son of the living God," Peter answered with zeal. Jesus went on to say he'd answered correctly, but not on his own. God had given Peter the answer.

Peter—*Saint* Peter—stands in for many of us: devout,

sincere, and almost completely mistaken about people and God. Which brings us back to two boatloads of fish from God. In response to this miracle catch, Peter fell down on his knees and cried, "Get away from me, Lord, for I am a sinful man!"

When it comes to this fishing story, every sermon and book and article and commentary I have ever come across presents Peter's fearful response as appropriate, prescriptive, humble, and good. "When in the presence of the mighty Jesus," they explain, "you should tremble in abject fear."

Peter, whom we know was always wrong (comically so, if you allow yourself to smile when reading sacred literature), was suddenly so terrified of the presence of the Divine, so jarred by the miracle, he begged the Lord to exit the boat even before Jesus had demonstrated he could walk on water.

But why should I suppose Peter's impulse had been right this time? Why would I think Peter's reaction to Christ *here* had been the right one but the ear-chopping thing was crazy? His actions had always been impulsive, his perspectives narrow, his theology needing constant dismantling and rebuilding. More often than not, when Peter did or said something, it needed to be undone and corrected.

Why do we not shake our heads and sigh at him as he cowers in the boat, "Oh, Peter, ya doofus. Stand up."

And why would the very next sentence have Jesus saying to him, "Don't be afraid," if being afraid *was* the prescription?

On what basis do we think that being afraid of God is the key to getting goodness from God? Why would we gather to sing to such cosmic psychopathy?

Perhaps even now you're getting nervous, wondering if it's okay to stop fearing the one who always opens conversations with, "Don't be afraid." Almost as one fears letting his or her guard down around a dangerous man, this business of removing fear from our faith feels like leaving ourselves at risk. Perhaps it has more to do with Bible verses, since we could all pitch in several about fear being part of what faith even means. After all, "fear of the Lord is the beginning of wisdom," as the proverb reads. I find most of us don't realize we've made fear the middle and end of wisdom too. Nervous adults still following the rules as toddlers do, for the same reasons toddlers do. We attempt being good for Dad to avoid a spanking, rather than to live well, to grow up. We do this and call this "wisdom" rather than the wrath mitigating it probably is. Some of us gave up on this faith long ago, because we outgrew a mental state that makes choices based on not getting busted. Some of us *would* leave, but we're too afraid God might prove to be a cosmic spanker after all. Imagine the minds of those singing in church of love and joy, afraid of the very object of their singing. It's mentally exhausting and often spiritually gangrenous.

Peter was a Jew. And Jews have always knowingly affirmed that God is aware of everything. As in nothing slips divine notice. One of God's traditional nicknames is *El Roi*, "The God Who Sees." (*El Roi* is pronounced "El Ro-ee," in case you thought ancient Israel might've looked to the heavens and called for Elroy.) God told the prophet Samuel, "I don't see things the way people do. People are stuck with appearances. What their eyeballs show them. I can see all the way inside." This is to say Peter's tradition taught that no one ever fooled God with their performance or achievements or Sunday best. No one ever tricked God into being kinder than God intended to be. No one ever incurred God's wrath by becoming less convincing. God's unlimited seeing is a big part of what makes God *God*.

And yet Peter, knee-deep in seafood, seemed to have thought the bounty of fish was given to him because God had yet to read his file.

"Get away, Lord, before you figure out who I really am and regret your kindness!"

If there is a mantra of the ashamed, this is probably it: *If only you knew.*

Peter acted like a terrified child, but because of our conviction that fear is good—holy even—we assume without justification that Peter got this thing right. *Be afraid. Be very afraid.* And if you don't walk around genuinely feeling it, you need to learn to conjure fear as a way of proving your devotion. Preach that people must be afraid of God in order to get God to tell them there's no need for their fear. Get people to fear God's randomly applied justice, like tornados and cancer, so they can live in fear that they don't live in enough fear. Because who knows—God may fill the boat with fish, or God may sink it to teach a lesson. Stay anxious. Your daughter may be born healthy. She may not be born at all. Depends on what point God wants to make. Stay nervous. If a good thing happens, you're owed a bad thing. It will happen when you least expect it, so remain tense. And by the way, God's judgment about that night back in college when you made a move on your buddy's sister is still pending. God Loves you, but that encounter did not go unnoticed.

But . . .

What if being afraid of God is as wrong as telling children to get away from Jesus? As wrong as swinging a sword at an enemy's head to "protect" the Son of the Almighty? As wrong as telling hungry people to go find food on their own?

What if God doesn't want us afraid, but we've so stubbornly assumed human beings can only do right if kept under threat that we can't imagine another way?

And what if the reason the divine voice is always heard saying, "Don't be afraid," is because there's ultimately no need for fear, and that it might actually be bad for us?

I know, I know—there doesn't seem to be much left of our faith if fear of divine disappointment and consequences are extracted. Wouldn't it be arrogant of us to think we'd become *less* afraid in the light of the Divine, rather than more? Well, if we're ready to get on with living the lives given to us, we'll need to recognize that Love cancels fear just as catches of fish cancel empty boats. And only when that fear is cancelled can genuine, honest life be lived.

2

PFJ

ON THE WAY TO THE BEACH a few years back, we saw an enormous billboard overlooking multiple lanes of highway. Pictured along the top of the giant rectangle was a storm cloud, with a huge Caucasian hand protruding from the underside. The hand was pointing at us all, the thumb and forefinger extended like a pretend pistol.

It read, "Jesus has your number. REPENT NOW!"

I felt angry and embarrassed. I began to imagine conversations leading to the decision to rent the billboard. I pictured an evangelism committee in some dank church basement passing around the concept art, which was endorsed with eager nods of approval before they finally segued to a discussion about how much church money they'd be throwing at this "ministry" to beachgoers. I felt angry that thousands of people a day were being told Pistol-Finger Jesus and my Jesus were the same.

I wondered irritably for several dozen miles, *Which of us can be wooed to God by threat? And to whom exactly was their Je-Zeus supposedly speaking? All drivers or just liberals? Those who enjoy a good IPA here and there, or strictly those with footed fish on their bumpers?*

God Loves you, losers. Accept it or be shot at.

I got over it after half an hour or so. But I'm sure there were other drivers who never did. Because for many of us, this is the god we grew up fearing. And we hide and estrange ourselves from what we fear. The Scriptures explain that Peter did. Adam and Eve did. Most of us still do. We hide from whatever threatens us or disapproves of us or wants to harm us. At the very least, we attempt to anxiously perform ourselves back into good graces. Or we get over it thirty minutes later and do what we want at the beach, having left the gaze of angry PFJ miles behind.

We don't want to be close to anyone who thinks badly of us, let alone a god whose mood is negatively altered by what we do. There is nothing more frightening and terrible than a god whose disposition we can sour with our humanness. The god who, when presented with the reality of our weaknesses, seems caught off guard by the power of these weaknesses. Like a gasping mother who walks in on her kids trying out some new potty talk despite their being commanded to quietly watch *Little House on the Prairie*. How dare you! She is powerfully oppressed by the least powerful beings in the house.

Some of us feel compelled to argue for this god. For the

goodness of this god. That fearing this god is what makes us take this god seriously. Some of us insist that when we say the word *fear*, we really mean *respect*. There's a world of difference, though. I respect my mailman. But if I am only respectful to my mailman because I think my disrespect might trigger his righteous indignation, then I have simply folded my fears behind a vocabulary word. Respect and fear shouldn't ultimately look anything alike. Especially in light of God's command not to fear, how disrespectful it is to continue being afraid!

But this idea that God wants you to be afraid of him isn't going anywhere because of a few paragraphs trying to convince you to the contrary. Faith seems dysfunctional without it. How else would we sinners be impelled to practice the holiness this god calls us to unless confronted with this god's terrifying volatility? Isn't the threat of a wooden spoon to the rear end how my mother kept me and my brother from beating the snot out of each other? Isn't it fear that holds the house together?

Yet, what fool thinks the bank robber is inspiring the bank teller to generosity by pressing his pistol to her forehead?

When PFJ yells, "STOP IT!" from the roadside, he is not yelling, "Fundamentally change!" *Stop it* doesn't mean "change who you are." It doesn't mean "become aware of a greater reality than you're settling for." It means "quit doing whatever you're doing because I disapprove of it." So then all we gotta do is carry on with our unapproved behavior on the other side of the billboard. We're not growing up. We're just avoiding PFJ.

I would gladly help fund a billboard that spoke more to the non-anxious, servant Christ's heart:

Jesus has your number. Pick up the phone; he's calling. Hello? He already knows your junk and what you really believe. None of it scares or angers God, even if your junk makes churches uncomfortable. Relax. Stop letting God's calls go to voice mail. Wanna go fishing? Hello?

I suppose the verbiage would need tightening up for those reading at highway speeds.

Here are some words of wisdom from the section of the Bible called Proverbs. I submit that they reasonably apply to God if they apply to the humans that God made.

Make no friendship with a man given to anger,
nor go with a wrathful man, lest you learn his ways
and entangle yourself in a snare.
—Proverbs 22:24–25

Whoever is slow to anger has great understanding,
but he who has a hasty temper exalts folly.
—Proverbs 14:29

A soft answer turns away wrath,
but a harsh word stirs up anger.
—Proverbs 15:1

A hot-tempered man stirs up strife,
but he who is slow to anger quiets contention.
—Proverbs 15:18

Whoever is slow to anger is better than the mighty,
and he who rules his spirit than he who takes a city.
—Proverbs 16:32

A fool gives full vent to his spirit,
but a wise man quietly holds it back.
—Proverbs 29:11

On one of those hidden-camera, "what would you do in this situation?" reality TV shows a few years ago, they set up people by giving them too much change. The cashier at a grocery store was an actor, and when customers paid in cash, they were intentionally given back larger bills than they should have been given. Cameras watched as customers walked away, counting and realizing the discrepancy, and then deciding whether or not to go back. Some customers went back to return even just a dollar. Some took back ten. Some people walked off with their bounty, and when interviewed said that they shouldn't have to rectify someone else's mistake and were fine with enjoying the fruit of another's blunder.

One man, after realizing that too much cash had been put in his hand, went back to the register to return it. The show's host caught up with him in the parking lot, revealing the setup and congratulating him on his ethics. The man was asked what made him willingly go in and lose money, even though the mistake wasn't his. The man said with a sheepish smile, "Well, I was raised as a Christian . . ." At this point I was thrilled that integrity and Christianity were having their vows renewed on national television. Score one for J team. But the man kept talking. ". . . and my mother always told me that if I didn't do the right thing, I would go to Hell."

The man may very well have been an honest man. But honesty wasn't his motivator. He did the right thing in order to avoid the consequences. And this does not necessarily a good man make. It was simply keeping the volcano dormant with an offering. There's nothing particularly inspired about what any of us do when it's done to keep ourselves out of harm's way.

Imagine successfully explaining away any sort of punitive consequence one might receive from God, so as to quiet the most fire-and-brimstone preacher. What if, for the sake of argument, we suddenly knew for certain that nobody gets eternally tortured in the afterlife? Does the man go back inside the grocery store to square up? Do we still do honest work and refuse to forge signatures or lie on the time sheet or smuggle home packs of printer paper or objectify our coworkers? Do we stop upholding vows and promises, stop telling the truth, stop making right decisions in the face of hardship? To whatever extent we begin allowing ourselves to do this or that in the absence of punishment, we reveal that we weren't changed as much as frightened. It seems to me only a cosmic child would look at the fruit of fear and call it holiness.

Threatening people does generally garner less bad behavior in the immediate. I know this (albeit untheoretically) because I have kids and an occasional short fuse. But we don't get better people in this arrangement, ever. We get worse people, because we get performers who inwardly fantasize about behaving differently than allowed. Which, for many of us, inevitably makes us gamblers in some measure. We start seeing what we can get away with. We start pushing the proverbial envelope. We start to get accustomed to having an inner universe that's entirely at odds with the outer one we portray. And when lightning doesn't strike, we try a little more. And then we try more. And then we create sophisticated ways of hiding or justifying the eventual expression of the unchanged interior. This is commonly known as a hypocrite. And before you and I get our pistol fingers out and start naming hypocrites we know: Does anyone create hypocrites at a higher volume than PFJ and the church of fear management?

When a man is penalized for honesty he learns to lie.
—Criss Jami

Peter had the one and only Jesus the Christ in his boat. And, unless it was omitted by the Gospel writers, Jesus didn't aim pistol fingers at him. Peter heard only his own voice judging and condemning, and like a lot of us he assumed it was the condemnation of the Divine. I try to remember *Satan* is a Hebrew word that means "accuser." I have to be cautious when assigning that role, because if I'm not careful I can look at a pointing finger and not realize it's my own. If Satan had gone on vacation for the last thousand years or so, I'm not sure we'd have noticed. We're enough *satan* to ourselves as it is.

Christ didn't affirm Peter's declaration from his frightened cower. Instead, he told Peter to *relax*. And Christ tells you and me to relax as well. Because God must know at least as well as seasoned employers that though fear may create immediate results in the workplace, in the long term it works against the organization. It creates not only anxious duplicity and division but also bitterness. We don't enjoy dancing when we're doing it because our feet are being shot at. And let's be honest—bosses who intimidate for results are prayed against. Everyone wants him or her replaced and celebrates when that supervisor is terminated. Many of us have done exactly this: fired PFJ as our boss because, as far as we've been presented, that god's attitude sucks. People aren't leaving church because they're too busy. People are leaving church because they're tired of being told anxiety, criticism, and trauma keep Heaven's lights on and God happy. They've gone to dance where no one is shooting at them.

Instead of feeding on the fear of a quivering self-flagellator, the Christ told Peter that his fear was out of place, and then Jesus invited him to come along and see what he was about. Later he said he'd build the church on Peter. This wasn't a mafia threat of being mixed in with a building's cement footer. It was actually a beautiful metaphor that, among other things, was about the kind of people who would shoulder the movement to follow Christ. Though it was a metaphor, Peter didn't apparently understand very well at first.

But we all are slow studies. Grace and peace to us all as we reconsider that our fears—and fears about fears—are out of place. The little anxiety center woven into the fabric of our gray matter is for survival in the wild, not salvation at the feet of Peace. How will we ever come to life if we're still, even through our spiritual practice, trying to hide from pain and death?

Perhaps we should, as Peter did, watch how Jesus interacted with a woman who fully understood how good it is to be known.

3

Apocalypse of Love

JESUS WAS TIRED. So was the Samaritan lady working to fill her pitcher with some noonday water at Jacob's Well. Never a big respecter of social taboos, Jesus stomped on a handful of them and looked this woman in her eyes and asked her for a drink. She sighed. Men were always asking her to serve them.

There was a way of things, and this man—a Samaritan-hating Jew, so far as she could tell—was apparently not up to speed. She pushed back on the request. "People like me don't do stuff for people like you."

This was when things started to get interesting. Jesus explained that his request for a drink was actually somewhat of a ruse. Maybe like when Inspector Clouseau tested Dreyfus by asking what his code name was, and Dreyfus called him a lunatic because he had no code name. Or maybe like when God yelled, "Yoooo-hoooo!" to Adam and Eve when they were hiding in the Garden, despite God being a pretty good people finder. Jesus revealed to the woman that he didn't actually want anything from her, but desired for her to *have* something instead. "Living Water" was how he put it. Something to quench a different, deeper sort of thirst. Allowing that they were both speaking in metaphor, she admitted she wanted whatever this was.

"Then go get your husband," Jesus said, without subtlety or the comfort of metaphor.

The story reads like a scene in a saloon, where a stranger walks in and quickly shows himself to be at the very least interesting, and then downright peculiar. The well was a place the woman could use to avoid reality, and yet reality is exactly what she was suddenly talking about, because this man was willfully terrible at small talk.

The woman's eyes widened. Rather than explain that the topic of her many husbands was none of the stranger's business, she said she had no husband to go get. Jesus agreed. "Yep. He's not your husband. The other five were . . . but not this guy you're shacked up with now. You're right."

The woman's stomach twisted. Down to two remaining labels for the man revealing her personal business: private investigator—maybe a previous husband was trying to prove himself not at fault for the marriage falling apart—or a prophet.

She tried to change the topic to religion. This is a favorite side road for religious people when real life jumps out in front of the car. It's amazing what truths can be obscured with a debate about religious traditions or correct interpretations. I've

seen thieves confronted who, in just a few sentences, can get you arguing about whether or not Adam had a belly button.

The woman pried open an old dispute about where God wants people to pray and sing to him from. Jesus graciously allowed her to run with the slack, then explained God isn't really beholden to, or perhaps even interested in, human veneration systems.

"There's going to come a time," Jesus said, "starting now, where real worship of humanity's Source won't be about this place or that place, this group *but not that group*; it will be about the Spirit, and about truth."

Like Peter in the boat listening to Jesus preach as they moved toward the shore, she could sense something profoundly different in this man's words. She worked up the courage to discuss in a roundabout way the suspicion that was boiling up inside her.

"We await Messiah. He will explain these things to us," she said. A question mark was drawn on her inflection.

"I am the Messiah," he said.

When Peter was confronted with *El Roi*, The God Who Sees, he immediately wanted to get some distance. He had to be told not to be afraid. Told to stand up and realize he couldn't hide and there wasn't any need to anyway. His reaction betrayed how uninspired his understanding of the Divine was. He thought God discovers things by degrees; like an old man squinting at you as you approach, God recognizes you more as you draw closer to his rocking chair.

After composing himself at Jesus's invitation to stop fearing, Peter left his fishing net and became a fisher of people.

The woman was also confronted with *El Roi*. Was also shown that, though bellied up to drink away her shame alone at the only bar in town, she was known and invited to live as profoundly as anyone else. She left her water pitcher by the well and ran back into town to become a bucketer of people.

She isn't recorded as being afraid. She seems to have liked being found out by the one unthreatened by knowledge of her backstory.

She went home to celebrate her revelation that judgment and Love are, despite what shame and fearmongering insist, the same thing. Why didn't we make *her* the first pope and call Peter "The Man at the Lake"?

You and I learned God Loves us but—*BUT*—like one who regrettably signed some contract years back that he can't get out of, God must judge us with such disorientingly harsh and unrealistic judgment that no one can do a single good thing and the Love stuff doesn't really have ultimate relevance. We learned, frankly, that God's Love is something much less than God's fierce reckoning. That only the latter is important to remember as you tiptoe through a day.

But this woman was known, and it hadn't cost her at all. Much the opposite, it had freed her. Love had judged her. The judge had Loved her. The truth had set her free. Now she was trading pretense for Spirit and Truth, running through her judgmental little town inviting others to experience the same.

"Come see a man who knows everything I ever did and was good to me anyway. Is this Messiah? I think it is!"

The word *holy* means "set off to the side" or "special by comparison." But what if the church wasn't just holy in its purported rightness in a wrong world—or even in properly managing its sins while society gets swept away in them—but by its not penalizing people for being honest? Surely that'd be something special on a planet of pretense, performance, and hypocrisy. What if there was no divulgence that could scare the church because the church celebrated seeing people as its God does, as beings who come alive when they are seen and accepted anyway? Truly that would make Christ-following different from—set apart from—other religions, including Christianity as we've come to know it. Any religion can demand sanctioned behaviors built atop suppressed guilt and shame and the fear of being found out. And they all do.

Would The Way and The Truth and The Life be offended if Christians established their church to be a (the?) safe place where people ran home afterward and said, "I told them exactly what was going on and it cost me no inclusion! In fact, my inclusion seemed to be *enhanced* by this level of honesty! Come and see!"

Or shall we all double down on the idea that lying about who we are keeps us lovable? Will we continue to cower in our boats and call it Good News?

⟷

In the book of Genesis, after the creation narrative of nothing becoming everything, we're presented the story of two nudists whose lives consist of gardening and sex. The rules? Do whatever you want, but avoid the Granny Smiths.

The result of their disobedience provides a foundation for traditional Christian doctrine: There is a propensity for human beings, from very early on, to do that which is prohibited. To defy on impulse what Wisdom lays out as necessary for life. *Original sin*, as it's been dubbed by some, despite that doctrine tending to make sin too central to *who* we are, rather than it being what nobody gets out of *doing*. Kids steal cookies. Teens use one another for sex. Adults build and expand on the first two. "All have sinned and fall short" is how the apostle Paul put it, though he wasn't trying to make everyone feel like garbage as much as he seemed to want to get some of his arrogant friends off their high horses.

Otherwise sane people routinely do what is bad for them in the singular and in the plural. It's always been this way. Genesis tells us in broad strokes about our individual contributions to a species systemically tainted with foolishness and regret.

When they realize they have acted rebelliously, the Scriptures depict Adam and Eve as suddenly noticing their nakedness. They feel ashamed. But if the text were referring to their mere *nudity*, the scene would be unintelligible. Their literal nakedness was God's idea, remember. I'm persuaded a different sort of exposure is in view.

When they sewed together fig leaves, they weren't inventing clothes. They were doing what you and I always do when we have something about us that we believe could estrange us; they were devising a way to control the other's impression. Putting a little something, a fig leaf, some income, witty banter, an in-ground pool, Bible recitation, varsity, the 5.0-liter exhaust package, cleavage, or biceps, between us so you have less of an opportunity of feeling badly about the real me, whoever that is.

This is to say the first effects of the first sin in the Bible aren't moral, they're psychological. The church often teaches sin as though Adam and Eve ate the fruit and then started an arsonist's porn site. But it was something far deeper than misbehavior. These perfectly peaceful human beings became concerned, perhaps *obsessed*, with veiling selections of their person in order to control the other's thoughts. They obscure, they *sham*—a word whose root can be found by simply adding back its *e*—and then the text goes on to show them hiding behind trees when they hear God coming.

Get away from us, Lord. We're sinners. If only you knew.

⟵⟶

Do not judge from mere appearances;
for the lift laughter that bubbles on the lip often mantles
over the depths of sadness, and the serious look
may be the sober veil that covers a divine peace and joy.
The bosom can ache beneath diamond brooches;
and many a blithe heart dances under coarse wool.
—Edwin Hubbell Chapin

The most winning woman I ever knew was hanged
for poisoning three little children for their insurance-money,
and the most repellent man of my acquaintance
is a philanthropist who has spent nearly
a quarter of a million upon the London poor.
—Sir Arthur Conan Doyle

Do not judge according to appearance,
but judge with righteous judgment.
—Jesus, John 7:24 NASB

⟵――――――⟶

The word *Hell* in the English language puts us in mind pretty quickly of a place of punishment. A location apart. The word stems from a Proto-Germanic term, *halja*, which means "one who covers up or hides something." It has the further original sense of something buried or hidden underground. From Greek the early followers of Christ borrowed the word *Hades*, both a netherworld realm and the name of this realm's god. Hades comes from *a* and *eido*, words that negate and mean "see," respectively. *Hades* is, roughly, "out of view." Pluto, another name for Hades, is similarly known as the god of the hidden underworld, specifically the god of earth's buried minerals, and is what we named the coldest, most distant, hardest-to-view rock in our solar system.

Hell is, at its etymological roots, a thing or state at odds with being seen as it really is. A thing unreached by light, and the misery its resistance to light creates.

The story of the primordial humans in the Garden isn't just about doing that which was forbidden. It's about all of us, from the beginning, sewing together our own Hell, our own system of hiding and suppressing and pretending, to see if we can pass as lovable since we're sure we're not. From the very beginning, really great people become so afraid that they become obsessed with themselves. Once it gets in your head that you may not be lovable, your entire internal budget is spent on compensating for that. And there's not much left over for loving others when you decide your own value is a variable.

As long as we can remember, we've lived as though the whole truth about ourselves is a liability to what we cherish most: unmitigated connection to others and to Other. And so we hide, cautiously peeking out from our layers of social, economic, educational, hierarchal, sexual, religious flora, keeping hidden the parts of ourselves detrimental to inclusion. We hide what's *hide*ous so we can appear not to be. Just as Carl Jung taught, we cram the liabilities of our flaws into the back storerooms of our minds where even *we* can't get at them, then go on living the fig-leaf pageant. We hide from each other. We hide from ourselves. And, however irrationally, we hide from the God who sees all and loads the boat full of fish anyway.

With a straight face, many of us who live this way call ourselves the people of truth. We even argue that we have it and others don't. But what is truth? We deride Pontius Pilate for asking Jesus such a question before the crucifixion. Yet I wonder if perhaps the man was looking directly into the camera when he said it, because it's you and I who need to answer, not Christ.

In the New Testament Greek, the word translated *truth* is the word *alētheia*. With an *a* at the beginning to negate, the second part is *lanthano*, which means "to cover or hide." Truth is simply that which has been unhidden. It's not a proposition or a winning argument. It's just the way things really are underneath. To be a people of the truth is to be a people about what's real. Who ask, seek, and knock to get at what is. Who dig past years of sediment until the shovel pings on bedrock. Who reward others who, even when it's uncomfortable or threatening, do the same.

Apocalypse, where faith traditions unanimously seem to believe everything is heading, is another word that has to do with revealing. What else would a book of Revelation seek to do? The most genuine apocalypse is when you and I and our society get truthed. What was hidden in the house is shouted on the roof. Light stripping away the shadows.

All this persuades me that Christ can't be interested in perpetuating fear systems that drive us to think almost exclusively of our own interests, of heading to the well alone while claiming to know from what mountain God wants to be worshiped. Christ, who was born and murdered naked, invites us into an awakened union with the Divine, a life lived with deepening sensitivity to the Spirit who saturates all that is. A way of being marked by our uncovered, unpretended, honest-to-God, naked truth. You know, the way things would already appear if you could see like The God Who Sees already sees.

> *Reality has not to be invented, it has to be discovered.*
> *It is already there. Hence science discovers,*
> *and true religion also discovers.*
> —Osho

A people of truth have a tough shift to make, because once you and I understand that being afraid always makes us hide, we can't go on inadvertently incentivizing that hiding in the name of our truth. We all have to accept that every action, every inaction, every thought, every true intention, every suppressed doubt and rage and desire to satiate our many hungers and lusts, is already known and is in plain view. It's known about me. It's known about you. Accepting this fact, that we are wholly seen and wholly Loved, is how we begin to understand what Love can really do. A Love that is judgment and truth and apocalypse and de-leafing and so many other things that, if even painfully, draw us from our shams and into life.

Fearful creatures hide, and hiding creatures are liars, and fearful, hiding creatures strain to Love anyone but themselves because remaining hidden takes up a lot of energy. Isn't this why so many of us are done with church? They handed us pants at the door and said, "This is no place for honesty. Here's our What We Believe statement." Many of us simply can't find enough evidence that the truth about Christ and the truth about ourselves is what we're after.

Your garbage probably bothered—and still probably bothers—mom and dad. A teacher. Your spouse. Your former spouse was perhaps the most bothered by it. The pastor and the elders and that lady in the prayer circle all voiced their distaste too. So consider that your life is very likely the story of how you've hidden your world from each of these people, while they have been hiding from you. We've all learned that even the most unmitigated train wrecks among us can look convincingly enough like good, put-together folk if given time to work out the show. I once had the unique privilege of hearing a mother wish she was as good and godly as another mother on the far side of the sanctuary. She pointed at her, with that recognizable blend of envy and disgust, having no idea that the other mother had been in my office a couple of weeks before to tearfully vomit her crippling doubt and insecurity all over my vinyl couch.

So, now consider that faith isn't something you pile on like yet another layer. We're already crushed under the weight of years of layering, each stratum another failed act. Consider, if even experimentally, that faith is nudity. A stripping of the layers— the fig leaves—and the release of their falsely securing duplicity. Consider faith not as the pretense of holiness, but the holiness of pretenselessness. Holiness as unhiding from the one who sees, and from those others who follow.

If you listen closely, "Don't be afraid" is the first thing God says to you every morning. Listen, it's there. You may not recognize it because it's not shouted or growled or popping up as a breaking bad news alert on your phone or as loud as the idea that your fear is what keeps your whole identity glued together. But it's there. And it's terrifying. And it's good. And perhaps your simple response could be to stand, your net and your bucket and your fig leaves at your feet, and to say, "Okay," a fair variant of *amen*.

NOTES

PART TWO

The Beauty in That Hideous Thing

Our strength grows out of our weaknesses.

Ralph Waldo Emerson

4

Life sucks

I KICKED OFF MY SANDALS and carried them into the woods for a barefoot prayer walk. It was exceedingly spiritual. Gandhi-like.

A few dozen steps beyond the tree line that faces the rear of the church building, my piety was placed under review by a swarm of spiritually antagonistic mosquitoes. They enshrouded me like the hash-mark cloud forming Pig-Pen's dirt aura. I waved my hand calmly at this distraction as I sought to pray and center myself. I imagined this was how spiritual masters would tend to a parasitic invasion, smiling and gentle. *Now, now, little ones, run along.*

Three or four minutes later I had descended into rigid, maniacal slapping. I'd even tried punching one particularly brazen mosquito for landing on my eye. My own blood zigzagged down my temple. My frustration was about to boil over.

Closing my eyes, I decided to pray. I sighed a resetting breath and whispered into the sylvan air a prayer to God:

"God, would you alleviate the annoyance of these mosquitoes so that I might focus on you? Amen."

A harp-strummed breeze blowing the bugs away at "amen" would have been a nice touch. Or Maya Angelou handing me a can of Deep Woods Off. Nothing like this happened.

Wiping my brow of sweat, blood, and the disappointingly low body count mashed against my scalp, I walked on moderately resolved and recentered. A sage in the forest.

The mosquitoes followed. Scads of new recruits joined the cloud as if God had gotten my request exactly backward.

I persevered. I was Bruce Banner, keeping my rage at bay, waving restrained, ineffectual swishes into the air as the swarm strafed my ears, their high voices taunting me.

I have walked this path dozens, maybe hundreds of times. Often the day after preaching, to wonder if I meant everything I said. I've spent hours on these leafy trails asking God to give me the maturity I lack, to show me what to do about the ongoing challenges in all my relationships, to address the gap between what I am and what I want to be. I've said the words out loud. I've thought them, too worn down to hear myself say the same crap to Heaven again. I've written my prayers in my journal and have been amazed how, years later, my petitions are identical. *God, why do I still not have better relationships with family, friends? Why do I feel like a fraud? Why am I not developing spiritually? What must I do . . .*

⟵―――――――⟶

Weeks before this scene I had caught a turtle in our church parking lot. She appeared to be relocating to our church's retention pond from some other secular pond in the neighborhood.

When I picked her up to take her to the water, I noticed she was covered with leeches. Twenty or more, attached to every soft spot on her body.

It was clear she needed my help and the leeches needed to be stomped into the pavement. Out of selective compassion I pulled the leeches off her one by one. I then gently placed the anemic little reptile in the water where she swam away free of parasitic oppression.

Later that same evening I felt two small bumps on my waist, right at my belt line. A closer inspection in the bathroom revealed what appeared to be a couple of eight-legged watermelon seeds. Ticks. Both of them were dining uninvited on my blood. I had apparently brushed up against some foliage while dealing with the turtle.

Then I saw my scalp in the bathroom mirror. It was riddled with bites. Dozens of them, pink and stretched tight. The mosquitoes had launched a sneak attack as I'd tended to the turtle.

Add to all this that one of my children had picked up lice at school that week. The stigma is worse than the reality, but the reality is bad enough. Bugs trying to live off my child without consent. My wife, armed with comb and flashlight, had spent several hours fighting to make our children lovable again.

I stood looking at myself that night after the turtle rescue, the mosquito pimples on my head, red freckles where the ticks had been, the fine-tooth comb that came with the lice removal kit on the side of the sink, remembering the leeches on the turtle. An unscientific hate was simmering in me. It had already been simmering in my wife. At one point in the delousing process, she had asked in exasperation, "Why would God create lice?"

Typically I prefer questions about simpler things like the Trinity or capital punishment. I don't pretend to know why God would see fit to make parasites. Especially if God only had, as the story goes, six days of making. Though many of us love God's creation, we hate these particular members with righteous disgust.

After some thought I'd shrugged my shoulders at Kristi's question. Who knows why God gave these damnable things life?

←—————————→

So on that day when my barefoot prayer walk was spiraling into the abyss, Kristi's unanswered question was still hanging in the air with the mosquitoes.

I couldn't recenter anymore. My piety and my veins had run dry. I was back to wishing there was a way to murder these insects slowly, painfully. The whining cloud circling my head began to obscure the sun. I started using my sandals as weapons, slapping them together and saying through gnashed teeth, "How do you like that?! Get some! GET SOME!"

Gandhi wept.

I gave up and started back for the church, furious at the universe. I had set out to pray, after all, not rob a bank or kill dolphins. *Pray*. My motivations entitled me to at least a squirt or two of Heaven's DEET.

Where prayer is concerned I long ago stopped expecting, let alone demanding, to hear an English-speaking male on the other end of the line. I don't hear God speak. But that moment, barefoot and seething, was one of maybe two times in my life I felt like I had.

"*GOD!*" I demanded as I swatted spasmodically on my way back to the indoors. "If I am to take you seriously, why can't you do something as simple as relocate these mosquitoes?"

In response I heard, *Because I want you to acknowledge how loathsome it is living primarily as a self-interested taker.*

5

GiVE

LIKE MOST EVERYONE, I suppose, I have an overwhelming capacity to choose my own interests over everyone else's, even as I claim to love them.

I didn't require audible divine intervention to deduce that parasites suck. Who doesn't already know all villains are takers? The bad guys are always plundering for their own cause, always in it for what they can get out of it, disguising their true motivations along the way.

After lunch at a restaurant one Sunday afternoon a man came up and said, "I just wanted to say, you have the most beautiful family." I was flattered.

We traded back and forth on what brought us to the area, the weather, all that. He was very kind. And then something happened to his voice. It transitioned from a normal inflection to a commercial baritone. A plastic fatherliness. He took a step toward me, his eyes fixed like weapons, and said, "You know, friend . . ."

He was stuffing his business card into my hand as he cupped my shoulder. On the card was the name of a multilevel marketing firm, their slogan said something about "dreams" or "the sky's the limit" or whatever.

". . . you're going to find there are times," he continued, "when taking care of this wonderful family of yours isn't going to be easy. You're going to need an opportunity to increase your wealth and achieve your dreams . . ."

My stomach got tight, like I imagine it does when a man finds out the woman who is coming on to him at the bar is a prostitute.

The entire conversation—all the compliments and interest in my life—was nothing more than bologna wrapped around dog medicine. Kindness as the folding table for a huckster to hawk his wares.

The tick had gotten his mandibles in stealthily and painlessly.

And we don't thank ticks for their painless invasion any more than we thank burglars for not waking the baby.

It wasn't that the guy was trying to recruit me into his business that made me feel like I needed a shower. It was that he was trying to do so in a way that made it appear as though *my* interests were his chief concern. I would have considered it neutral to positive if the guy had just come out with it. "Hey there, I'm inviting people to have conversations with me about my business because, well, it's how I put food on my table. The business model is such that I benefit from having solid people working for me, and frankly, the structure serves you well too if you work as hard as I do. Here's my card. Can we chat to see if we think we can trust each other?"

But instead, he tricked me into thinking he was kind and that I was special.

This is an important distinction: My issue wasn't that it was self-interested. It was that it was self-interest disguised as Love. Like a shallow opportunist flatters one to the bedroom. It reduces human interaction to an effective sales pitch with a commission. And since we assume this of people, of course we assume God can also be bought.

Takers are the worst, fine. Those don't-be-selfish sermons are a tithe a dozen. The remedy religion offers to the alleged sickness of selfishness is to shame selfishness and reward even the most plastic altruism. Fake it till you make it. The result is often parasites who feel secretly ashamed for their continued parasitism, who therefore dress up in charm and charity. Leeches who get good at romantic poetry.

Demonizing selfishness doesn't cure us of selfishness. You know this already. It only makes us lie about what we're doing as we continue to behave selfishly. In other words, shaming self-interest forces people to expend even more energy on themselves in order to polish their presentation. It makes us twice the tick we were, because now we also have appearances to think about.

> *Do not* merely *look out for your own personal interests,*
> *but* also *for the interests of others. Have this attitude*
> *in yourselves which was also in Christ Jesus.*
> —Philippians 2:4–5 NASB, emphasis mine

←—————————→

Religion, and most of what we dub *spirituality*, posits the elimination of selfishness as the pathway to personal transformation and holiness. After all, it's our brazen selfishness that made God so angry with us in the first place, right? Become selfless, and in so doing, become good. Bad people are selfish and good people are selfless, so choose this day whom you will serve.

I should admit this has been the point of dozens of my own sermons, though in hindsight I suspect I never once believed myself. I extolled the holy loft of austere selflessness as Christianity's trajectory, while my chief—if well-*veiled*—concern was that the congregation would think my sermon on the issue had been first-rate. "Think nothing of the self," I'd intone while obsessed with how everyone thought I was doing. It's a funny thing preaching on selflessness and googling your name afterward. Like most people, I failed to recognize the subtle, more worried voice whispering constantly under my sanctimony.

Who but me is looking out for me?

There's a deep, jittery terror that if I become anything other than a well-liked taker, it's suicide. There just isn't enough kindness, or cash, or forgiveness, or time, or rides to work, or patience for listening without talking, or credit, or available Saturdays to spend packing the neighbor's U-Haul, or benefit of the doubt to go around.

What if I give and don't get? Oh dear God, what if I give and don't get? *Who but me is looking out for me?*

In the absence of sedating answers, I'll generally choose to protect me and extract from you.

But, crap. I can't allow others to see my extracting selfishness. That would also count against me. Nobody likes ticks. *Loathsome*, remember? So I must look out for me but make it look like I am thinking of you.

To this level of consciousness is preached the vacuous moral of selflessness. And in response to this preaching we get anxious, selfish persons who learn to master the art of *sucking incognito*. I'd argue this is why we call each other "person"; in Latin *persona* literally means "mask." We're robbing one another.

Saint Paul said evidence of the Spirit includes things like love, joy, peace, patience, kindness, goodness, faithfulness, gentleness, and self-control. This kind of verification, that a human being is on track and growing, was put forth by the guy credited with writing about half the New Testament.

Previously he'd been quick to offer as proof of his spiritual aptitude things like his education, his circle of friends, his accuracy, his pedigree. With time, he began to see all that as silly. He even called it excrement. Now it was this: *the fruit of the Spirit*. Hard, measurable, and beneficial evidence that something more than our own ego or desperate survivalist is at the helm. The confirmation in Paul's mind that the Spirit of God is working in someone's life is a list of words that have to do with *others* being the main trajectory of our intention. Others made beneficiaries of my existence. This is something even illiterate people who don't go to Sunday school or thump Paul's writings can participate in.

He used an image of fruit hanging off the branch or weighing down a vine, above ground where others can see and enjoy and know for sure exactly what kind of tree they are dealing with. It should be pointed out Paul listed no potatoes of the Spirit.

Fruit is something freely offered by the plant to birds and squirrels and bugs and Dole. It gives the fruit away as an accessible gift to whomever or whatever needs it, with no demand for reciprocity. It blesses the world around it with no guarantees for itself. No promises. No thank-yous required. *Take the fruit and enjoy it. Don't want it? I can respect that. You'd rather let it rot? That's okay, I'll simply grow another fruit tree where you stomped it into the ground. Maybe you'll eat from that one. You owe me nothing, for my life doesn't come from you. I make fruit either way. It's what I am.*

But there are other facets to the metaphor of fruit that aren't as glorious and lofty as they are basic biology.

The fruit is hanging from a tree that wants to live. Living things want to stay living things. The fruit literally gives away the DNA of the tree, its identity and its own survival packed into its offering. The tree's fruit is for others, but its own existence is in view as well. It's never tried to hide this.

The tree *requires* water, soil, sun, and protection from urban sprawl. It gives, but it also has its own welfare to consider. Any tree that decided to be all give, sweet fruit without seed, to produce while shunning sun and rain, would be an idiot. A dead, withered, fruitless, idealistic, idiot tree.

Consider the message of God and mosquitoes and welts on my person: human selfishness isn't to be eradicated. It can't be. It's to be observed and properly calibrated. If we try to eradicate it, try to moralize the impossibility of selflessness, we get deception masked with altruism. And we hate this. We despise clever duality intended to benefit one but not really the other.

Acknowledging the impossibility of selflessness takes a ton of pressure off of us. There's always self in my actions. I am in everything I give. Despite the negative connotations to the word, everything we do is a measure of selfishness. Too much self and I've become a tick or a devil. A user who sees the world as its pharmacy, its feeding trough, its relief. However, attempt to obliterate the self altogether, as religion often insists and pretends, and now I'm a frustrated liar who has needs and desires hidden from view, from others and perhaps even from myself. A living being pretending to be something he or she isn't: inanimate, or God. This polarity also creates monsters we loathe.

The paradox of attempting selfless living is that it drives the focus unendingly on self: self-abdication, self-discipline, self-condemnation, all require self-measurement and subsequent self-adjustment. Self, self, self, self. That is, the so-called selfless folks are often the most self-obsessed people I've ever met. In trying not to be as loathsome as a swarm of mosquitoes crashing a prayer walk, I focused even more on my performance and in many respects became even less attuned, less loving, to the world around me. It takes a lot of energy to disappear something that won't leave. Maybe this is the reason one of the definitions of *pious* is "unlikely to be possible"; it isn't. And in the absence of real magic all we're left with is sleight of hand.

Paul knew this. "Let thieves no longer steal," he said to his Ephesian brothers and sisters. "Instead, let them serve others with those hands." Religion says cut off a thief's hands. Christ inspires us to grab the impulse to take and harness it to serve. To recalibrate the taker itch and use it to bless. A sword bent into a garden hoe. It's always been this way.

When we learn that the live stream of intel that selfishness can provide us is a tool, *not a terminal disease*, our ability to love one another in truly insightful, meaningful ways reaches a whole new level. We don't have to spend so much time and energy condemning ourselves, bemoaning our lack of progress as a spiritual person or even as an adult. We don't have to involve ourselves anymore in the ongoing insanity of comparison with others. Now we have the data we need—like most Kingdom things it was there all along, right where we already were—to employ Love and Joy and Peace and Patience and Kindness and Goodness and Trustworthiness and Gentleness and Self-Control for the mutual advantage of others and self. And we don't have to lie to one another, because we're no longer under the fearful delusion that there's anything wrong in benefiting in some way from things that involve others. We're in this together, connected and honest, unafraid of seeing and being what we were made to see and be.

6

There is a free lunch

DURING THE ICONIC SCENE known as the Last Supper, Jesus said something he probably didn't intend to be routered into small church tables. He distributed to his disciples some bread and a cup of wine and said, "Do this in remembrance of me."

This moment is Christ instituting what we now variously refer to as communion, eucharist, common table, the Host, etc. It's an ancient ceremonial meal—for the title "meal" there's a whole lot missing from the food pyramid—that calls to mind for the participants the broken body and spilled blood of Christ.

This is Christ mysteriously/figuratively/concretely/ritualistically giving himself away. In the final scene before dying on a Roman execution stake, he passes this food to his friends and says, "Do this and keep the way I did it front of mind."

In John 10:10, Christ says, "I came that they may have life and have it abundantly."

In other words, had folks asked, "Jesus, what's your agenda?" his response would have been something like, "To give life. Buckets of it."

Maybe ticks are on one extreme of the spectrum and Christ is on the other. I wonder how many of us think of God as a taker who has the power to make taking seem good. Listen to the words of some eulogies, the way God allegedly takes loved ones for his own purpose, and you get the idea that the Almighty can be as tick-like as he wants to be about anything, but you can't feel bad about it.

I grew up thinking God demanded things. *Every*thing, frankly. Like a cosmic revenuer who comes to collect if he comes around at all. But Jesus, by his own admission, came to *provide* something. People take or leave Christianity. But I've seen them drawn to Christ for at least this: Christ doesn't take. Christ gives.

The Hebrew word *Ahava* in the Bible is translated "love." At its root (*hav*) it means "to give." With the modifiers added (*a-hav-a*), it means "I give."

When faithful people speak of God's Love, they are speaking of God's unlimited gift of Self to humanity. Thus, the term *unconditional love* is redundant. Requiring that conditions be met is a demand for payment. A self-interested clause: *I will give myself to you if (or after) you satisfy my terms.*

This isn't *Ahava*.

Ahava Love is the risky, vulnerable, uninsured act of donating what I prize most. Me. And Christ gives this living, breathing, bleeding Self away in a figurative meal and then on a nonfigurative cross.

> *Love is unselfishly choosing*
> *for another's highest good.*
> —C. S. Lewis

The very Jewish, Hebrew-speaking John wrote the words "God is Love." He was saying that this was his experience of the essence of the God who made him. Not just loving, but by nature *is* Love. God is by his essence perpetually choosing others' highest good. This is very different from the idea of the folded-arm ego who created me in order to worship and please him or else. Instead, we're told that at the center of the universe is a continuum of benevolence. A bottomless well of good for all. The eternal anti-tick who even Loves ticks.

I don't know what you learned about God and his expectations of you or his feelings about your worth. But if you think that anything you have done or haven't gotten around to doing can disrupt God's nature, you're just being a bit unintentionally arrogant and altogether ignorant. Arrogant because you came to believe the idea that you have thwarted eternal Love with whatever dumb thing your little self did or didn't do. Ignorant because, well, if you knew what Love really is, you wouldn't spend so much time trying to earn it. But be of good cheer . . . ignorant, cocky people are just as Loved as anyone else. You and I can't get out of it.

One term used for the bread of communion is the *Host*, which I can now see is a pretty solid name for the thing on which parasite-ish folks, such as you and I can be, are invited to feed. The Giver gives. We take. This doesn't seem to be an offensive proposition for Christ. Mortals offering food to the deity is a premise for another religion. The tradition of Christ eagerly embraces that we're the ones who get the meal.

Perhaps there's as much relief for you as there is for me in this: Your selfishness isn't evil. It's assumed and even largely catered to. You and I the baby birds, and God the brooding mother. Grace still amazes.

Our relief comes in understanding that our selfishness is not out of place as much as it's out of tune. Maybe a lot out of tune. Maybe just some. The one who tunes us seemingly affirms that we aren't capable of self-sustaining and that we are not hated for this. This weakness becomes a strength, a basis for inspired good for the whole species. Bread and wine, food and drink, to remind us that we're to have a healthy, balanced self-interest at the table in order to be as connected—to commune—as we need to be.

You love all the things that are . . .
Never would You have made anything if You had hated it.
—Philo, to God

7

→

The opposite of Love

How can I look like something that doesn't look like anything? Michelangelo seemed convinced God had a righteous beard. The movie *Dogma* put forth Alanis Morissette as the Almighty, sans beard. Morgan Freeman and George Burns both reminded us that older men look more like God than the rest of us do, while the movie *Exodus: Gods and Kings* suggested that the Lord is a British kid.

God is variously depicted in the Scriptures as totally invisible, unapproachable light, fire, smoke, and generally non-formed. John, in the same section where he shared that "God is Love," also made the bold assertion that "no one has ever seen God." So we must be made in the image of an essence. We must be the *likeness* of Love.

Less an image for cloning but more a Being to mimic. *Ahava*, writ small.

This might explain why we are so inspired by the seeming otherworldliness of acts of Love. When we see someone living with the arrows of consideration pointing outward, one person giving him- or herself to another, something at our core recognizes it as the highest, holiest good. It's a glimpse of our true essence. Even if Gary never paid you that $300 he owed you, you'll probably still find a way to celebrate his *always being there for you* at his funeral. *Ahava* is what matters most to us.

Mirror neurons in our brains show us that we experience other people's experiences in our own being. Anyone who has cringed when someone *else* has a spider crawling up their leg understands this. We are wired to feel beyond the boundaries of our own self. Our stomachs go in knots for a person grieving. We cringe at another's lacerated knee. Our hearts race to see a child rescued. We feel elated when the underdog hits the game-winning home run. We, the observers, simultaneously the participant.

We're made not to just watch, but to connect and care and coexperience. It's our nature, because we're made in the image of a Love that's always finding ways to unselfishly choose for another's highest good, no matter how buried this nature becomes under a given culture's superficial enchantment with outperforming others.

The Buddhists long ago began teaching the principle of *bodhicitta*, which is essentially an enlightened mind that doesn't only *know things*, but is fully attuned to its natural, untaught, hardwired default setting to be able to feel others' feelings. While the modern human thinks of him- or herself on the basis of what has been accomplished or acquired, the ancients were seemingly more dialed in to what is most true: we are Compassion by nature.

The Christ insists we are compassionate because we come from Compassion. Chips off the old Block.

God created humans in God's own image,
in God's image God created them;
male and female God created them.
—Genesis 1:27, my rendering

How many of our favorite stories move us because the protagonist gives their fortune, their reputation, their comforts, their position, their life, for others? Even if they resist to the very end and then finally relent, doesn't it feel like the highest payoff?

Even after it was debunked, how long did that story continue to show up in our social media feeds about the mother bird found dead by the fireman after the forest fire? Her babies survived because she'd apparently given herself as a living, winged firewall to save her offspring. We continued to share it, knowing that even though it wasn't true, somehow it wasn't false.

And who wonders why firemen eat for free all over town?

A boy lifts a wall during an earthquake to save another kid, himself dying as a result. Who wouldn't call the child a hero of the highest order?

Who's against the woman who gave her car to a poor family and just started taking the bus?

Who doesn't think something mature and wonderful and inspiring has just happened when a toddler decides to share her cake or Legos without being told to?

Who doesn't feel something warm in their hearts when they hear a couple sharing wedding vows? "In sickness and in health, rich or poor, when times get tough—I will always give you me." Only the cynical, the wounded, and the distracted DJ don't feel a bit elevated inside, more alive somehow.

Something echoes inside of us that this Love is the truth running under our terror. If only for a second, our soul feels reminded and smiles. And yet we forget. You and I both will, if we're not awakened to what lies beneath, spend most of today forgetting what matters most to our being. We might spend our whole lives banished from our true selves, wondering why others seemed to have found what we could never find.

⟷

We've come to refer to the moment when Eve took the forbidden fruit and gave some to her husband as The Fall of Man. Well played, ladies. I suppose it did require an enchanted snake to trick Eve into eating what God had prohibited, whereas with Adam it only took his wife handing it to him.

The serpent was an interesting choice of animal to make the villain. Doubtless the snake was feared by the time Genesis was written for all the reasons a snake is feared today. But the primordial picture of a limbless animal might suggest that, before serpents carried with them so much lore and psychological baggage—and before they came to be used to *make* baggage—they may have been considered a mere stick with a face. A benign little reptile tube, cast in Genesis for appearing, like many things we regret later, harmless.

How much more unthreatening could an animal be?

A serpent is not endowed with limbs. No hands and feet used, like Adam and Eve, to serve. Serpents don't do much of anything for anyone other than themselves. The serpent "was more crafty than any other beast," according to the story. That's smooth-talker crafty. Smooth talkers talk smoothly because they want to get something from you without you feeling it. You smooth talk to *get*, not *give*. The serpent has no hands to make, create, or assist. It has no feet to travel alongside others. It can't hold, carry, comfort, pull, push, build, plant, fix, cook, or do anything in the sphere of providing work or service. It can only live in holes dug by others, absorb the sun but provide no warmth, and also hiss, strike, and eat. Even its hug is about something else.

This is why we say, "Give me a hand." It means, "Help me." No one says, "Give me a snake." Maybe a few churches say that, but that's a different topic.

Snakes cannot *Ahava*, making them utterly unlike Christ. They're self-prioritizing and dialed almost entirely to "self."

This is the creature that dupes two mentally sound people, made in the image of Love, to act like nervous idiots. A creature whose entire MO is "me." And perhaps this is why the story of Adam and Eve deserves another look for both the devout creationist and the staunch  biblical antagonist: Maybe its historicity isn't the point. At least not the main point. Maybe the point is that you can bring down human history by getting Lovers nervous enough to principally love themselves.

The subtext of the Genesis creation story might be this: We get worried we're not going to be okay, until we're finally not. We worry we're going to miss out, be mistreated, get hurt, die. This fear makes us shortsighted. Whoever planned a birthday party in the back of an ambulance? This shortsightedness, this blindness, makes me turn my Love, my regard for highest good, in on myself. It's like this for all of us. It's not simply evil. What a lazy word *evil* can be. It's fear, having reversed the stream of Love back to its own heart to protect itself. It's the bastardization of Love, turning it in on the self for survival. Oscillating fans turned Shop-Vacs. The bad—*the evil*—we commit is Love that we were to give away but instead reserved for the self. Little wonder why Saint Paul once wrote that the base of our being wars against our spirit, and that the two are in conflict. I don't think he meant our sweet tooth works against our diet in the ice cream aisle. We have a backflow of Love that kills the very thing we're trying to protect. Compassion and Grace are, in part, a way of looking at evil and straining to see that it's actually fear. Love all out of tune.

Who can blame us for getting all out of whack?

At this very moment your body is warring against disease. You are managing resources to make sure vitamins, minerals, oxygen, and a list of other unpronounceable elements get to where they need to go for maximum health. You are internally managing waste. You are currently regenerating and repairing, in your limbs and your organs and in many of the thirty-seven trillion cells that have you pieced together. Add to this the unthinking work of things like balancing in your chair, your readiness for sexual reproduction, digestion, breathing, and thermoregulation, and you begin to realize how busy you always are taking care of you. Then there is unconscious evaluation of safety. The instant risk assessment on a flight of stairs, maintaining balance while cleaning gutters, analyzing others' body language for threats. And then the billions of dollars of industry based on our desire to be found physically attractive, or just clean. It takes work. More work for some than others.

Physical, social, emotional. We spend a ton of resources on our own well-being. Just underneath our sophisticated vocabularies and designer jackets, we remain to some degree coiled, ready to spring. Fight or flight, that primal readiness that worries itself away from harm. Locked and loaded. Kill or be killed. Life, at its ground floor, is the vigorous effort of not dying. This is the brain's chief responsibility.

Let's not judge it. Just observe it happening. These things operating in the background are there for our benefit. There's an appropriate selfish interest in us required to live, to propagate. I'm saying that most of this is God's idea. And it works.

The problem for so many of us is that all this doesn't operate in the background. It becomes anxiety overwhelming the foreground. It becomes the delusional belief that our surviving moment to moment is *who* we are, like thinking the sole point of the family vacation is the car running fast and being shiny. It's out of proportion and ruins the trip.

I spoke to a woman recently about some of this that was playing out in her life, as I perceived it. She dismissed my observation as too pathetic. She even wrinkled her nose. "I'm not anxious. I'm a grown woman." A month later she had chosen to replace the word *anxious* with *vigilant* and could see clearly that the snake had talked her into pouring most of her Love energy into protecting herself from pain and difficulty. She admitted she was perpetually afraid.

Maybe it sounds *too* pathetic for all of us at first. But the next time you get angry at a coworker or loved one for lying to or about you, the next time you fly off the handle at someone's erratic driving or bad customer service or lateness to an appointment, the next time you realize you've been thinking for weeks about a sideways glance or a bad review you received and it's haunting you and you keep mentally marinating about how you might be able to transform that person's opinion of you, the next time you find yourself enjoying the dog pile on top of or the excommunication of someone who's been a troublemaker in your life, ask yourself what else those thoughts and fantasies could be but the fruit of self-defensive fear. A fear that others are going to spoil your life and therefore need to be attacked, rallied against, or fled from. Scapegoats. Monsters.

I worked with a man named Jack in a sales office. And I also worked with a younger man named Martin. And I worked with a young woman named April. Jack was great. But I hated Martin because he was far more attractive to April than I was to April. Jack was several years older than me and was a literal legend in the company for his sales and leadership. I enjoyed time with Jack for many reasons, not the least of which because this time spent made me feel like I was sharing in his power. And when we were together, I often relished—I'm talking moaned with delight—when Jack spoke about how terrible Martin was at his job. I used to ask if he'd heard about Martin's poor performance, or if he'd heard the stupid thing Martin had said in the sales meeting. I used to bring up Martin, even doing a bad impression of him without provocation at lunch or in the car, just to get Jack to say or do anything I could interpret as his disgust for Martin. My admiration of Jack was charged by his attacking Martin, and my insecurities were medicated with Martin's blood.

You can imagine how wobbly this relationship architecture became when Jack began dating April and they became very serious, very fast. I was forced to find new friends to gossip with, to form common enemies with. And of course I had to quell the romantic dissonance by deciding April was a sleaze.

Love is always flowing, but pain and fear get it flowing in reverse so strongly that this self-love becomes a necessary hatred for others. Others are no longer the objects of my compassion. I am, nearly exclusively. Relationships are rated based on their ability to provide me relief. Different actions and attitudes are directed at those who provide it than those who threaten it. Friends and family are categorized by annoyances, how validating they are, etc. It's a complex, justified system of me disproportionately loving me while manipulating everyone else into either doing the same, or becoming something for me to stand on. A pope once said the opposite of Love isn't hate, it's use. He was right.

The opposite of Love is love.

Faith, then, may be the suspension of the survivor impulse even as it clangs away in our self-interested brains. Faith reroutes Love, gets the pipes flowing in the right direction, mindful of its own mortal limitations but not turning those limitations into cause for laying siege to the universe's resources to avoid pain. Faith is the way we trust Love enough to recover from being users.

A prayer about all this might sound like, *Dear Love, I need help getting my fear back into the backseat so that my true nature, which is a reflection of your Nature, might do the driving. Help me recognize opportunities today, with those I know and don't know, to not be afraid to give myself away.*

I'm not saying this is magic. I'm saying that the Christ teaches us to look at the world and observe our mind's fearful response to it. And with this observation we can begin, in faith, to determine, *I won't be afraid, because being afraid makes me very much unlike myself. Instead, I will route my Love in its best, most initially terrifying direction: mostly toward the other.*

Think of the Christ as coming to assist us in our crucifying the part of us who takes his or her cues from snakes and ticks. If his cross was in large part an act of Love, then our cross might be understood as the ongoing act of uncovering this same Love from deep within ourselves. Forgiven people turning sin into goodness, darkness into light, by accepting an invitation to be what we really are: temporarily confused Lovers made from Love.

> *I think we all have empathy.*
> *We may not have enough courage to display it.*
> —Maya Angelou

8

It's always something

A COUPLE OF YEARS AGO I was speaking at a student conference held at a midwestern university. Each day there was a morning session and an evening session, one of which I would lead; the middle part of the day was set as free time. One particular day there was a dodgeball tournament held on the tennis courts, one of many justifications for parents signing medical release forms before the church vans headed out for the week.

I participated in one round of the tournament. As I waited my turn I stood near a chain-link fence. A young girl approached me and asked if I could give her advice on a particular relationship wrinkle she couldn't iron out. Her seeking me out for this speaks to her desperation and youth.

She got about three minutes into her story and one of my young teammates yelled out, "Mr. Daugherty, we're up." I asked the girl if we could pause for a moment so I could make good on my first commitment—injuring minors with a ball—and then I would come back and listen some more. She obliged.

I ditched my flip-flops and opted to play barefoot. The late-June sun had heated the court's surface to a considerable simmer.

It wasn't excruciating, but I had to keep my feet moving like one of those desert geckos that do yoga poses on the hot sand. Once the game started I stopped thinking about my feet because I was thinking about branding children's faces. I was doing well by anyone's but a Child Protection Services agent's estimate.

As I dodged a last ball chucked at me with generational prejudice, I felt my foot slide in the strangest way. I looked down, and it appeared the soles of my feet had come loose. They were squishy and misaligned. I panicked, getting hit in the eye during the distraction.

I started limping toward the sidelines. Pain. Pain and panic. This was a new kind of pain for me. It was bad and weird and it was alarming. My feet were beginning to swell. Then bloat. An achy heat radiated up to my ankles. The soles of my feet were freakish, gelatinous blisters. *Good lord,* I thought. *I've cooked myself.*

I returned to my previous place at the fence, moving like a man three times my age. This was going to be a really crappy day on a college campus, where walking was how one got everywhere.

And as though the tape had only been paused, the young girl picked up where she had left off on her relationship woes. "It's not that I'm *mad* mad at him. Just mad. You know. Like just mad. He just always, you know, like he never . . ."

I listened the best I could, but remaining interested in what I felt was best suited for her diary was becoming extremely difficult. My pain and concern were increasing by the minute.

Then I heard a deep *whir* in my right ear, followed by instant fiery agony. A large wasp stung my ear in response to my leaning up against the part of the fence in which his satanic family had built their nest. I shrieked in a way not in keeping with traditional notions of masculinity. Pain rippling across my face, I could feel my heart pounding in waves through the right side of my head. I gritted my teeth to compose myself while the young girl interrupted herself to ask, "Ew, are you okay?"

I nodded with a strained dignity. "A wasp just stung me in the ear."

"Oh my god," she said. Then, after a beat, she continued her talking.

My feet had melted off, my ear an inflamed everything bagel, and she just kept talking.

But I wasn't listening.

I knew she was talking because I could see her mouth moving. But I wasn't listening.

I had stopped caring enough to even be disappointed in myself for not listening. I was trying to think of how I was going to get back to my dorm. She was pouring her heart out, probably, and I couldn't have cared less. It was me I was concerned about.

Once again insects teaching me that it's always me I care so much about.

The young girl, bless her heart, God love her, sweet thing, was suffering heartache and disappointment. But all she could allow herself to see was her own desperation for relief. Exactly like I was doing. Two people suffering, unable to appreciate anything outside their fixation on their own misery—unavailable to care for each other because all the caring in our hearts was monopolized by our own pain.

It seems like most of us think we're in something like agony all the time. A low-grade misery, at the very least. So of course we can't even listen to each other. We can't put others' interests ahead of our own. We'd like to. Love is great. *But I got nuthin'.* Something in us knows what beautiful lives look like, and we'd enjoy living that way. Once this or that gets straightened out, then I can care about you. Once these circumstances pass, I'm all ears. Once I have extra money, more energy, I'll be there for you. Once I work through my bad childhood, this audit, this check engine light, you can count on me.

Later.

Not now.

Because right now I need affection, attention, affirmation, consideration, care. So unless you are here to have as much compassion for me as I am trying to aim at myself, please leave me alone.

This is probably why we think we'll be generous when we win the lottery. We're waiting for relief. We'll be kind when people are easier to be kind to. We're waiting for relief. We'll be who we really are once the pain and suffering and difficulty pass. Until then, I'm not listening. Not until there's relief.

The snake sells apples to this part of us, the part that suspects the center of the universe is scarcity rather than boundless Love. The part of us that believes deeply that there's a great Withholding on the throne instead of boundless Love. So we bastardize the *Ahava* in us, inverting it so that the Love we were made to radiate we now chiefly demand and collect. From bright, life-giving suns to inescapable black holes.

So when our tradition shows us the Christ as a suffering servant, one who was acquainted with grief and misunderstanding, who knew physical, emotional, relational, and familial pain, and yet also shows us Love, perhaps we're being shown that we don't have to wait. That we shouldn't.

Maybe our pain is a tool for understanding what we're hearing, rather than an excuse not to be hearing at all. Maybe rather than trying to get fixed, or to fix others, we should come to believe that our struggle is the means by which we understand one another, not the obstacle to first overcome before we are available to one another.

A friend of mine once said that the church is a great place to heal, but church *leadership* is a terrible place to heal. I really do see his point. But he meant the nonprofit organization that requires well-managed lives to well manage it. The real Church— that organism that can still meet when the power goes out and the building falls down and the preacher goes on vacation— is a people living the honest story of mutually experienced pain for the mutual healing of the species. The Body of Christ should be known for its affection and Compassion, not for winning Bible trivia, and for bandaging one another for both the sake of the other and for protection against falling into the bottomless pit of the wounded, anxious self.

Maybe I'm ready right now, with my bad knees and my depression and my out-of-whack budget, to really Love others as much or more than I'd want them to Love me. In fact, maybe I'd be less ready if I ever got all that just so.

NOTES

PART THREE

A Love So Basic

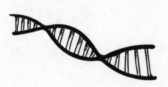

No act of kindness,
no matter how small,
is ever wasted.

Aesop

9

Do this—all of this

WHEN JESUS PASSED THE BREAD and the cup to his followers
and said, "Do this in remembrance of me," of course he was
talking about eating the bread and drinking the cup. But it's
interesting the specific phrasing isn't "eat this" or "drink this" in
remembrance of him. It's actually, strangely, unspecific.

Do this.

As if his handing them the
bread and the cup, symbols of his
self-sacrificial Love, are included in
the *this*.

If you watched someone hand
a hundred people money and say to them, "Do this," would you
be surprised if many of them understood it to mean more than
receive cash? Would you be surprised if many of them interpreted
the "do this" as meaning both giving and receiving money?

Jesus invited his pupils to remember him within the whole
scene: a room full of takers—being recalibrated to give more
of their Love away—were being given what they needed *and*
being told to perpetuate the giving of it for others.

We consume. We produce. Take. Give. Breathe in. Breathe out. Both. It's what we are, as endorsed by the Manufacturer.

> *God's gifts aim at making us into generous givers,*
> *not just fortunate receivers.*
> *God gives so that we, in human measure, can be givers too.*
> —Miroslav Volf

"Teacher, which is the great commandment in the Law?" asked a scribe who was subtly putting Jesus, a purported rabbi, to the test. Jesus responded, "You shall love the Lord your God with all your heart and with all your soul and with all your mind. This is the great and first commandment. And a second is like it: You shall love your neighbor as yourself. On these two commandments depend all the Law and the Prophets."

The entirety of the tradition hangs on Loving God and Loving others. And the quality of this Love of others is measured by nothing other than an awareness of how I like to be Loved. Selfishness isn't eradicated. It's the most important tool in my belt, if only I could learn to see it, and then use it, without shame.

During the Sermon on the Mount, Jesus offered up something that sometimes makes me wonder why our Bibles are so thick, our sermons so long: "Whatever you wish that others would do to you, do also to them, for this is the Law and the Prophets." Awareness of what I want is necessary to fulfill this. Well-calibrated selfishness is assumed, acknowledged, and leveraged. The whole Bible is me knowing what I want, and using that intel to make your life better.

Jesus's brother James wrote to his dear friends about their new lives and way of living. As he wrote out some course correction about their perpetuation of social hierarchy and relational superficiality, he included, "If you really fulfill the royal law according to the Scripture, 'You shall love your neighbor as yourself,' you are doing well."

Paul's letter to the Romans includes toward the end, "The commandments, 'You shall not commit adultery, You shall not murder, You shall not steal, You shall not covet,' and any other commandment, are summed up in this word: 'You shall love your neighbor as yourself.' Love does no wrong to a neighbor; therefore love is the fulfilling of the law."

The Bible in CliffsNotes: use your selfish awareness to Love others well.

It's as though Jesus comes to us saying, "You know how you're pretty sure, most of the time, how you would like things to go? How, when you screw up, you hope your intent will be considered far more than your actions? How you'd like others to talk to you, or not talk about you, when you're not around? You know how you love it when someone picks up the slack for you and you don't get the sense that you're now indebted to them? You know how good it feels, or how good it must feel, to be able to trust others entirely? You know how great it is to find out someone took the time to think through how something might affect you? You know how great it is to be honored, respected, and included irrespective of your performance or lack of it? Okay: Provide all this to other people. Give to others all these things you know you love receiving. In so doing, you will have fulfilled everything the Scripture was getting at."

The key to Compassion, to being what I am, is my selfishness properly adjusted. A tool to use, not a curse to be lifted. We can't help but Love, because that's what we are. But in fear of everything from terrorists to not having a prom date, we have aimed it toward ourselves. Love walks the old lady across the street or steals her purse, depending on its calibration. Once we see things aren't just generally bad or good, but inward and outward, then we have a real shot at being born again. Not into a world of self, but one of other.

This growing ability to recognize the self, and therefore, by humble extension, the other, feels pretty great. I like myself more when I am being what I am. For God's sake, let's not feel bad about that. Neither should we lie about it. It feels great to be what we are. Why else would Jesus have said, "It is more blessed to give than to receive"? He didn't say it's not a blessing to receive, let alone that it's bad. He said we're wired such that to have a few more of the arrows pointing toward others than ourselves is better, despite the whiny insistence of the vigilant internal mosquito who's commandeered the helm.

We consume the bread and the wine, and we, to an ever greater but never absolute degree, also mimic the Christ's giving of those elements. Giving his very self. "Do this." Perhaps there's no better way of knowing if you get the point of your human life than to come to minor in consumption and major in provision. Having a day-to-day awareness that the inner tick wants to focus on the self, yet subverting it by using its constant flow of self-interested intel as a way to know how to best understand, serve, and Love the other.

We are born with a great capacity for Compassion. To receive it as creatures who need it. And to give it as creatures who were made to provide it.

If we can just get the dials right. And that's perhaps a decent prayer for your morning routine:

God, Love, help set my dial. And like a good dad protecting the home's thermostat, swat my hand if I mess with it. Amen.

10

---------→

51%

UP ON THE MOUNTAIN Moses asked God to reveal to him God's appearance. God told Moses that this would melt his face off, give or take a detail in the translating. Moses would need to be shielded, so God placed him in a nook in the cliff side and shielded the little man. And there Moses was, hearing the roar of a hundred freight trains and the hiss and tumble of gravel raining down around him as the divine Presence blew by. And in the roar, God put into words what God was like. You just might find remarkable the first word God used. I can imagine Moses did.

"Compassionate."

This word *compassionate* in the original Hebrew is the root word for a mother's womb. A womb is a place where you are nurtured, protected, developed, wanted, eagerly anticipated, bragged on, surrounded, and cherished before you could possibly earn it. Where you are loved because you exist, not for anything like your achievements or your stance on gays or your take on whether stegosaurs had a stall in the ark. You are loved because Love loves you. You can't get out of it. To exist is to be the object of great Love.

It is after this pattern we are told we're created. We are like this, *essentially.*

Years ago, driving to Ohio in the predawn, I chugged caffeine while my family slept. Kristi was curled up in the passenger seat, her pillow wedged between her headrest and the window. The kids were bundled under blankets in the back. The temperature outside the van was a brisk thirty-four degrees.

When I noticed my feet were numbing in the cold, I made an adjustment to my dial. We had one of those posh multi-position temperature controls that allowed the driver, the passenger, and those in the back to have their own temperature settings. I cranked mine well into the warm red.

A minute later, Kristi stirred. She was also cold. With one swift movement she dialed her side up several degrees. Then she returned to her fetal curl, and then immediately uncurled again and adjusted the setting for the rear of the van where our children slept. She coiled up a final time and went back to sleep, her and the children warm.

When I was cold I warmed myself. Stimulus and response. The sophistication of an iguana.

When Kristi got cold, she warmed herself as well as the kids. Stimulus and higher, compassionate response.

This difference between us is typical.

At noon on Saturday my stomach growls. I immediately think, *I'm hungry, I want something to eat.* So I make myself something to eat. Stimulus and response. This is a fairly uncalibrated behavior because that's as far as the thought and action go. It's love, but dialed deep into the "ME" setting. There's a ring on my finger and children listed on my tax forms, but after over a decade and a half I still too often have the communal awareness of a man living on an island, alone.

At noon on Saturday my wife's stomach growls. Her first thought? *I'm hungry. It's lunchtime. I need to get the kids some food.* The love of self is the handy alarm bell announcing it's time to Love others. Not *selfless*, or others would suffer for the lack of awareness. And not wholly *selfish*, or the final result is the same. The needle on Love's meter should be kept at "51 Percent Others." On this depends all the Law and Prophets.

We are all born with a basic, biological Compassion. Its intensity might vary, but it's there in some measure within all of us. The mother in almost all mammalian species is able to make the interests of her offspring her own.
Their suffering is her suffering. Their thriving, also hers. Fathers have their own version, of course, so this isn't any sort of man bashing. Parental Love is ideally as basic as it is beautiful. But it may not qualify as necessarily inspired. For many people it's simply a biological framework. Survival of the species. A winning impulse. A construct.

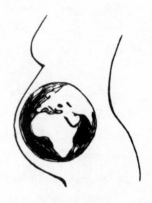

And yet this is the first, fundamental truth God is depicted as sharing with the captain of the Exodus. *Compassion.* Empathy. Motherly care poured out irrespective of the children's capacity to reciprocate. A rudimentary construct that at the very least promotes survival of the species. And to a greater degree this simple Compassion shows us what might just save the world. Look at the cross, at the Compassion for even those proudly dubbed the enemy, and you might be convinced it did.

To bear the image of *Ahava* in our limited way might be the task of taking what's already part of our basic biological framework and expanding it a little more each day. To include not just those we most easily give ourselves to, but to have our Compassion become so expansive that it begins to encircle the acquaintance, the stranger, the idiot, the ex, and even our enemies, growing to Love even them the way mothers adore their little angels and their brattiest little terrors.

> *Love properly understood is God—the font of all creation*
> *and the ultimate goal of all desires;*
> *God properly understood is love.*
> —Miroslav Volf

We all, even the most obnoxious among us, have the basic capacity to care for others. The easiest objects of our most fundamental Compassion are those we appraise as weaker than ourselves. Perhaps this is why Jesus put forth *the least of these* as an easy group to give ourselves to first. It counts. It's good. "Functioning mammal" is a fine start. It's in keeping with the design specs. And if we start there, and grow in our awareness of others' hopes and needs as we have grown so accustomed to knowing and focusing on our own, we can go from a Biology 101 level of Compassion and radiate it outward even to those who in their uncalibrated selfishness would right now do us harm. "You have heard it said love your friends," Jesus once said. "But I'll show you how to even love your enemies."

Being made in the image of Compassion is, for us, an invitation to learn to Love people because they exist. Period. To move out from under a love that's offered on condition of others' performance, and instead to take on a parental sort of embrace of people. To move through the day asking for eyes to see others as your own kids, whom you'd almost instinctively give yourself to, at your own expense. It may take us becoming old men and women to learn how to Love one another like they're our own offspring. So perhaps we can begin with a daily choice to set our dials of Compassion at "51 Percent Others" out of the conviction that we are, at the very least, always Loving the fruit of God's womb.

11

→

Love is in the air, and everyone breathes

JUST OVER SEVEN CENTURIES before baby Jesus was laid in a feeding trough, a man named Isaiah quoted God as saying that God's message would not return to Heaven empty. I imagine a divine boomerang where other deities don lightning bolts. What God pronounced as will-be-accomplished will circle back to confirm for all humanity that it indeed has been. The cosmic point will be made. The Word does not return void because this Word isn't a mere idea—it's Love, embodied at work subtly and hopefully all over the world.

In the Gospel of Mark we're told of a conversation that Jesus had with someone well acquainted with the laws and commandments, and the traditions that had grown out of them.

A scribe arrived and heard Jesus and some religious leaders debating. When the scribe saw how well Jesus handled himself in the exchange, he pitched him a question many rabbis got asked.

"Which commandment is the most important of all?"

Jesus answered him, "The most important one is tucked into the sixth chapter of Deuteronomy: 'Listen, O Israel: The Lord our God, the Lord is One. And you shall love the Lord your God with all your heart and with all your soul and with all your mind and with all your strength.'"

The scribe was already nodding.

"And the second one is like it, you'll find it in Leviticus," Jesus continued. "'You shall love your neighbor as yourself.' These are the most important."

The scribe believed his own endorsement was important, so he gave it. "You're right, Rabbi. You spoke correctly that God is One, and there are no others. That to love God with all the heart and with all the understanding and with all the strength one has available, as well as to love one's neighbor as oneself, these completely trump the entire ritualistic and sacrificial system."

And to the man, Jesus responded something like this: "Unlike your associates who delight in the members-only club, *you* are not far from the Kingdom of God."

But Jesus wasn't saying anything new. That's likely why the scribe was so immediately on board with it. In Jesus's response to the scribe he quoted from work written nearly a millennium before, and as a young Jewish boy, the scribe would have undoubtedly heard other rabbis, most notably Rabbi Hillel, saying the same thing.

> *What is hateful to you, do not to your fellow man.*
> *This is the law: all the rest is commentary.*
> —Rabbi Hillel, Talmud, Shabbat 31a

And what you hate, do not do to anyone.
—Tobit 4:15, Judaism circa 100 BC

The Compassion that made the universe is bubbling through the cracks of everything. All of us, everywhere, have it on our shoes if we'll just stop and look. Grace reaches outward throughout all humanity, tapping gently on our shoulders, whispering the most important things in our ears, inviting us to live deeply and beautifully before we ever hear it on the lips of an evangelist or in the text of a sermon. Every person you've ever met, and then all the other ones, are being invited every moment of every day to live in the flow of giving and receiving Love. Or did you think it was just you and me?

This I found surprising only when I thought God was mine. When I thought the message was for a select few of which I was somehow lucky enough to deserve to be a part, and the rest of humanity had to wait in line to hear the few good homilies available. But the Word doesn't return to the Word-giver void. This message is not impotent. Self-sacrificing Love is not a tenet for one group of us but is a way of describing all of us. No one is far from the Kingdom of God, any more than fish are far from water or birds are far from wind.

As the apostle Paul taught us, observe the wisdom of other traditions and note how the message of how we best Love one another is so ubiquitous; it's almost as if there really is one best way for all God's kids to act toward one another:

Hurt not others in ways that you yourself would find hurtful.
—Udānavarga, Buddhism

*Ascribe not to any soul that which you would not have
ascribed to yourself, and say not that which you won't do. . . .
Blessed is he who prefers his brother before himself.*
—Bahá'u'lláh, founder of Bahá'í

*This is the sum of your sacred duty: Do nothing to others
which would cause you pain if it were done to you.*
—Mahabharata, 5:1517, Hinduism

*. . . a state that is not pleasing or delightful to me,
how could I inflict that upon another?*
—Samyutta Nikaya v. 353, Buddhism

Do not do to others what you do not want them to do to you.
—Analects 15:23, Confucianism

*Tse-kung asked, "Is there one word that can serve
as a principle of conduct for life?" Confucius replied,
"It is the word 'shu'—reciprocity.
Do not impose on others what you yourself do not desire."*
—Doctrine of the Mean 13.3, Confucianism

Whatever is disagreeable to yourself do not do unto others.
—Shayest Na-Shayest 13:29, Zoroastrianism

*None of you truly believes until he wishes
for his brother what he wishes for himself.*
—Muhammed, "Al-Nawawi's Forty Hadith," Islam

*Try your best to treat others as you would wish
to be treated yourself, and you will find that this is
the shortest way to benevolence.*
—Mencius VII.A.4, Confucianism

*In happiness and suffering, in joy and grief,
we should regard all creatures as we regard our own self.*
—Lord Mahavira, 24th Tirthankara, Jainism

*A man should wander about treating all creatures
as he himself would be treated.*
—Sutrakritanga 1.11.33, Jainism

*Regard your neighbor's gain as your gain,
and your neighbor's loss as your own loss.*
—T'ai-Shang Kan-Ying P'ien, Taoism

*That nature alone is good which refrains from doing
to another whatsoever is not good for itself.*
—Dadisten-i-dinik 94:5, Zoroastrianism

*All things are our relatives; what we do to everything,
we do to ourselves. All is really One.*
—Black Elk, Native American

*Do not wrong or hate your neighbor.
For it is not he who you wrong, but yourself.*
—Pima proverb, Native American

To those who are good to me, I am good;
to those who are not good to me, I am also good.
Thus all get to be good.
—Lao Tzu, Tao Te Ching, Taoism

The law imprinted on the hearts of all men
is to love the members of society as themselves.
—Roman pagan proverb

All the world, all that's been made, is being called back to what it is: Love. And this returning back might well be called repentance. A return to our intended form, and to Who formed us. To come home to ourselves, and to the great Benevolence who spoke us into being; the shame and the shams that kept us apart dead and gone.

It is perhaps noteworthy that Christ didn't stop at proclaiming or adding his two cents to an already-popular take on the Golden Rule. Uniquely among teachers, after summarizing the entire message of God with it, Christ lived the Golden Rule to the very end. It's easy to tell people to Love others as they want to be Loved. Even easier to copy and paste several examples of different traditions who've said it. It's far harder to actually Love, to refuse to become the angry divide, even to the point of being murdered on a Roman cross—all because you know it will awaken what God has made.

No wonder Christ said, "Follow me." We've gotten all the use we can out of quotes. Now we get to participate in making sure the holy boomerang goes back with a solid progress report, written on the stock of our actual lives.

NOTES

PART FOUR

The Polarities of Control and Love

Compassion

mid-14c., from Old French *compassion* "sympathy, pity" (12c.)

. . . from com- "together" + *pati* "to suffer"

12

The amnesty of honesty

WHEN I WALKED OFF THE STAGE, half a dozen people told me it was one of the better sermons they'd heard. An older man shook my hand with his right, patted my shoulder with the left, and nodded at me, the signature Christian affirmation from that generation's men. I felt good about what I had said, and was feeling pretty good about what others had said about what I'd said. Who am I kidding? I was getting drunk off the compliments.

When Wade walked up to me, I anticipated his usual, well-spoken encouragement. His wife was a devout Christian woman, while he was a confessed agnostic with atheistic leanings.

Wade, a sincere man a decade or so my senior, as humble as he was articulate about his heavy skepticism, was someone I'd secretly taken on as one of my first evangelical projects.

He was shaking my hand and had made the effort to come to the front of the room to talk to me, and I was sure that he was as moved as he was convicted.

"That wasn't fair," Wade said, our hands still moving up and down.

I was confused. When I asked what he meant, he referred to how I'd ended the sermon. I had closed by referencing a poll that showed a vast majority of people, provided the opportunity to have a conversation with anyone in history, would choose God. Not only was this the most popular answer given, but it was also the most popular answer given by self-professed Christians. I had ridiculed this as sad.

After sharing the poll numbers, I declared that Christians, at least *real* ones, should know we have direct, unmitigated, unmediated, unrestrained access to God now. We call this prayer. I had said that we can and should already be having conversations with God. Why were they wishing to a pollster that they could?

"Don't you see, brothers and sisters, you can have this conversation today!" I'd pontificated in full accordance with what I believed I believed.

"Huh?" I asked Wade, pulling my hand back. "What wasn't fair?"

"That was a cheap shot, and it wasn't fair, Steve. You know you don't have that with God."

"Wait. What?" I was still making the internal switch from *bask* to *defend*. Wade continued.

"You know you don't have back-and-forth conversations with God like you and I are doing right now. You know how frustrating it is to talk to God even on your best day of prayer. How you wish you could sit down and chat with him and hear him unambiguously speak back. I don't think what you said was fair, it wasn't right, and I don't think *you* even believe it."

I was speechless. Not just because this was the first time I had ever seen Wade confrontational, but because I couldn't find a secure space in my mind to argue from. He'd thrown open a door to an unacknowledged room I'd dutifully kept my back to. He was pointing inside, demanding I see what I'd denied for Jesus.

I knew how to talk about the power of prayer, the interactions one has with the Lord when they are a follower, my personal relationship that far exceeded my youthful Catholicism that I relegated to empty ritual because that's what new Protestants are taught to do. I knew all the Bible passages, read a few books. I had a poster in my office that read "Make War on the Floor" and featured a man bowed down, prayer warrioring, which I think is the term's verb form.

The truth was, however, that prayer had been a struggle in every way.

The truth was, I sorta hated prayer.

I often did it begrudgingly, ashamedly, confusedly. Prayer made little logical sense to me and reinforced a terrifying sense that faith is no more than a one-way conversation exclusively reserved for anyone willing to suspend their disbelief. At times prayer even reinforced my deep insecurity of being rejected by the God who doesn't talk back. The absentee father who doesn't answer the phone but sends unsigned postcards from wherever he is. People speak of a personal relationship with Jesus Christ, but it generally functioned like a distant celebrity and a fan club.

I knew all this was in that well-lit room behind the door. But to admit it was, in so many terrifying ways, to part with my new identity, my heroes, to divest myself of my newly acquired tradition, to go cold turkey on the affirmation I loved being addicted to. To tell my church that I didn't like prayer and that it made me feel crazy when I did it felt communally and vocationally suicidal. So I argued and defended myself against Wade while trying not to notice I agreed with him on the inside.

And then days later I confessed to him that I agreed.

I agreed prayer was not at all to me what I alleged it was supposed to be, that it was illogical to me on a lot of levels and had never felt right. That while I knew some people who prayed and didn't seem to have these hang-ups, and others had stories I could only categorize as miraculously specific answers to the requests they'd made to God (I even had a handful, generally, I conceded), prayer wasn't for me as I'd preached at all.

There was plenty more I could have confessed about all this, but it was a few brave steps toward truth. And an interesting thing happened: I felt closer to Wade. And I *was* closer to Wade. I believe two beings are closer than they were as soon as the truth-obscuring leaves between them are shed. But feeling closer to an agnostic after admitting your own doubts about prayer probably isn't that surprising.

What surprised me was that I also felt closer to God. As though I had named the actual terms between us, rather than extolling what was supposed to be despite knowing its fiction in my own life, and had been rewarded for it. Who knows, maybe that confession to Wade was one of my better prayers up to that point.

In fact, I've felt closer to every one of the hundreds of others I have admitted this to. Not because I just happened to find the few people on earth who secretly thought the same as I did about talking to the Divine. But because prayer is, for so many people, a strange, seemingly fruitless, and ultimately undesirable part of daily life—they're left feeling secretly crappy and unspiritual about it. I found people need someone to understand this, not underreport it. To acknowledge without condemnation the reality, to not bury it in shaming either/or rhetoric.

I thought I was being loving in telling necessary truths rather than actual ones. But in my pastoral desire to dutifully strengthen the flock, I reinforced for most of us that we're excluded. That I am strong and you are weak and you need to hide your weakness if I/we are going to include you in our strong lot. My desire to look solid in the faith did what pretense always does: created a stage full of actors pantomiming truth—Jesus called these *hypokrites*, Greek stage actors—and an audience full of people who were a disconnected, gradually disinterested second class.

But honesty has always been more Loving than dogma. I've always preferred people tell me what they actually think, versus what they're expected to. The former is a bond. The latter is self-preservation.

Which means I already have the means by which we can be good friends—be connected and bonded in the way that we all long for, so long as we haven't held out for it for so many years that we've decided we want nothing less. In this moment, you and I have a means by which we can experience our fuller humanity, or more honest faith, if we'll just stop telling each other what we think we're supposed to say.

Compassion requires we accept what is true, not what must be. Compassion is unafraid of what it finds when it opens doors to rooms others deny are there. Compassion isn't offended or disgusted by what is revealed by picking up old logs and facing what's underneath. Compassion tells the truth, swallows the truth, accepts the truth, and rewards the truth, so help us God.

What a terrifying thing Compassion can be.

13

→

There is no remote control

I WAS FIVE, RUNNING THROUGH THE HOUSE with a blue towel tied at my neck like a cape. It was evening, the fluorescent light of the kitchen and the aerator on the aquarium gurgling. I was young Batman of the suburbs, with no mask, no crime to fight, and plenty of pre-bedtime energy to expend.

My dad staggered out of the back hall in his underwear, infuriated at not being asleep. He was working swing shifts as a young state highway patrolman. Mom had been shushing me, but Batman had awakened the real, exhausted crime fighter nonetheless.

I had not just woken him up. I had made him angry. Really angry.

We learned as young children that a person's mood—especially all the older persons—as well as their enjoyment of life, were a contingency. A contingency others controlled.

Your noise level, willingness to eat vegetables, punctuality, attention to detail, grades, room cleanliness—all these and more were the major determiners of your guardians' mood and how you might be treated as a result of that mood.

In other words, you've known most of your life you were in control of people, especially powerful people, and they were in control of you. And this inadvertent control stays with us into adult life and is well rooted long before we ever discover it happened. How much of what we say we "want" on a given day is actually whatever rocks others' boats the least?

My mom says it happened in less than a second. In an impulse of irritability, Dad grabbed my towel as I ran by. My cape jerked tight in my dad's strong hand, my feeble knot slipping open. My little frame spun like an Irish dreidel into the kitchen table, my forehead gashing open on one of the wooden legs. The rest of the memory is a whirling blur of my apologetic father holding me in his arms, carrying me into the brightly lit emergency room, surgical sheets as blue as my cape over my head, the sting of the needle as they injected a local, Dad holding my hand as they stitched me up, Dad petting me, Dad making jokes. Dad ingratiating himself to me, his five-year-old.

I had never seen my dad so upset, and then so accommodating, so willing to eat out of my hand.

I clearly remember his anger, which I had caused. But perhaps just as significant, I remember well the strange satisfaction of his remorse, *which I had also caused.*

I fanned the flames of this remorse, mindful in my five-year-old way that it was my hand on the dial of his guilt. I was punishing him, and it was working. A long history of a father and a son occasionally puppeteering the mood of the other was born.

When I walked into the front room recently, my son's socks were crumpled on the couch next to his shoes, his Legos, a book, and some trash from a snack. I bellowed his name, demanding he clean it up. I felt anger and frustration coursing through my veins. I would have said it to my friends like this:

"It pisses me off when the kids don't listen."

"The kids really infuriate me with their disrespect."

This is to say, I'm a grown man and my children have the power to dictate my mood. And they suffer for it, because I believe they've caused the suffering. They have wounded me, insofar as everything was fine in my world until their existence took from mine. So I perpetuate the silly, devastating lie that my children caused my upset. Worse, my children don't learn in cases like this the supposed moral value of a clean house or taking responsibility or being respectful or any such crap I tell myself I'm trying to instill during my tirades. What they learn is when Dad doesn't get his way, Dad gets angry.

I am losing my temper because I am not getting what I want, and in so doing allowing the behavior of children to govern my happiness. They aren't learning responsibility. They are learning irresponsibility because I am in charge of me and not doing a good job with that responsibility at all. I'm teaching in those moments that when they grow up, when they encounter something they don't like, they should blow up. Upset themselves as though controlled by all the world but themselves. This isn't them learning the value of a clean home, if a "clean home" even has any value beyond individual preference. (Whoever first said "cleanliness is next to godliness" was probably unaware of the hell they were unleashing on children forever.) When I throw a tantrum at my children for their performance, no matter how justified I think I am, I am teaching them to perpetuate the worst of childhood: Be crying, disempowered babies until the outside world changes. Then everything will be just how they want.

I transfer the teach*er* far more than the teach*ing*. Container *far* more than contents. Kids watch, rather than listen. My son didn't learn about picking up Legos. My son learned how to yell about Legos, and how to make it seem like it's someone else's fault.

You "made them angry" or "grieved them" or "ruined their morning," our parents and teachers told us. In some truly unfortunate cases, kids even heard parents or relatives tell them, "You make me sick." I know adults have their contexts too. After all, adults can almost be entirely understood as old children. But even old children can see that it's a disastrously stupid thing to hand young children, or anyone else, control over our happiness and be surprised at the ensuing dearth of bliss.

It's likely you and I both got into a few backseat turf wars as kids, slap fights with a sibling or a cousin about their encroachment on our side or whatever. Typically this would lead to locking eyes with mom or dad in the rearview mirror, their eyes framed like a livid ninja's mask. And then came the warning: "Don't *make* me pull this car over." Generally we straightened up at this. But more subtly we had reinforced for us that sinners run everything. The driver isn't driving when the kids *make* them pull over. The parent is at the mercy of the children. It's a major reason we had to go to bed so early. Not just because we were young and needed the rest. Our parents wanted control of their lives back for a few minutes before they went to bed and reawakened to our enslavement.

It's control the younger versions of us believed we wanted, and perhaps even thought we'd mastered early on. What kid doesn't love puppets? But by the time we realize that the inability of our parents to deal with all our untamable youth will generally result in our own misery, it's far too late to give the remote control back.

Once a handful of Jewish men asked their teacher for some prayer tips. One of them spoke for the group:

"Jesus, teach us to pray."

Jesus responded, "Our *Father* . . ."

Oh crap.

Good or bad, how we perceive parents of course informs how we see God. Parents and teachers are, quite concretely, our first gods. That is, the security of their happiness is probably how we view the security of God's. We think we've been made the custodian of both.

The word *anger* comes from the idea of strangling, of restricting. Probably because angry people are red-faced and panting like someone was just choking them. This is the term we use to describe God's feelings about us. He's angry at what we've done, or were too cowardly to do. He's got sequoia-sized veins swelling in his enormous forehead. He huffs. He curls his lip and shakes his head a little, disgusted and ready to let you and me have it. We have, according to our chosen vernacular, victimized God with our behavior. Just like we did our parents and teachers.

How many times in the last year have you heard that a person or a group has beliefs or behaviors that anger God? That God's wrath is kindled by someone's ideas and actions, the clear implication being God's mood was ruined by human activity in the same way your dad's was when you left your bike in the yard for the third day in a row. It's an arrogant message—that little you or little me can control the Lord of the Universe's ability to enjoy all that's been made.

God was having a great day until we arrived.

I'd say that makes us pretty powerful little transgressors. God in the hands of angering sinners. God as a showerhead raining down on us whatever temperature we dial up on the faucet with our behavior. A god that can hardly claim the *All* in Almighty, as I think about it. For so long I couldn't conceive of God without God being as angry as I've seen the men and women in my life get. For so long I didn't realize anger is about things happening to you, against your will. Thank God we can't do this to anyone who is actually *God*.

This is perhaps why it's so hard for some to respect the object of Christian faith. We depict God as one whose creations can dictate his state of mind. For people who believe humanity has free will, it's interesting to conclude humanity's *god* does not. For people who don't believe in free will, it's even more interesting, since God would be the one scripting the very behaviors that lead to God's own wrath!

Either way, no wonder so many people have left church. For similar reasons many of us moved away from home. Being responsible for powerful people's moods is too much to bear, so we pull away. Perhaps this is how distance makes the heart grow fonder.

There are numerous passages and entire stories in the Scriptures that highlight the wrath of God. Most of us couldn't understand the point of our faith, or the fundamental narrative of the Bible, without God's anger. But our understanding of God changes, deepens, broadens. Depicting God as angry is very likely the most intuitive and effective way to show that God is not indifferent. It reassures us that God is interested and involved and has taken notice of people victimizing others with their abuse of power. That the underdog is not forgotten, that it infuriates God when life is lived harshly and without sensitivity to the sacredness of life, as it infuriates a father when his kids beat each other without mercy in the backyard. However, as all of us develop, we should be able to see that the description says more about us than God. Perhaps more with regard to anger than any other feeling. Haven't we learned, as Dallas Willard insisted, that "anything you can do with anger you can do better without it"? Aren't we becoming more aware that anger is a physiological *reaction*, a primary emotion, a result of something being in the way of what you and I want? Do we really believe God's will gets overthrown, causing frustration/anger/wrath?

I would never tell someone how to feel. And if I did without realizing it, I'd apologize, because telling people what to feel is a dumb thing to do. Probably especially anger. I've been angry in the last forty-eight hours myself. And I see anger in others based on their experiences in talking about religion and politics and other important conversations, many of which haven't gone that well around the Thanksgiving table for years. I feel what I feel, as do you. But anger is not improving the world around us. If anger could do that, then cable news could save us all. Their uncanny ability to stoke rage and make us come back for it again and again is astounding but understandable; surely they present us all the frustrated talking heads and infuriated panelists so that we can get things fixed.

We can feel anger, and we will. But anger is an expression of our powerlessness—our lack of freedom or control for some period of time—rather than what it often pretends to be: our prescription for what ails us. Anger as a solution is not a winning strategy for anybody, God included. As we used to say in wrestling, and I understand we stole it from boxing: "Get your opponent angry, because whoever gets angry first, loses."

> *Go ahead and feel anger, but in your anger,*
> *don't let it make you sin.*
> —Paul, Ephesians 4:26, my rendering

If I suppose that God's anger is some "higher" version of my own, but called by the same word, then I'm compelled to make more emotional comparisons. If a person gets angry and behaves angrily, that person also very likely has the ability to be happy—elated even—and to laugh. Both are emotional responses to external stimuli. But the Bible never depicts God as having a good laugh. Why is it easy to imagine God angry and smite-ready when a kid drinks a beer on spring break, yet not laughing and holding his ribs when that same kid shrieks in unnecessary terror when her sandwich is torn out of her hand by a seagull? Are we really excited to spend eternity with a God capable of wrath and not laughter? A God infuriated by supporters of the other candidate, but who doesn't laugh at cat videos? If we're not feeling excited about spending forever with this emotional imbalance, we're probably too terrified to admit it. But it would be terrible. Absolutely terrible.

It's little comfort to read passages that depict God as "slow to anger." Because if God gets like I do, or like our moms and dads did, what's to praise about getting to that same point a little later? Perhaps it helps to visualize anger the way the old Hebrew seems to intend us to. The biblical phrase translated in English as "slow to anger" doesn't concretely say anything about *slow*, *to*, or *anger*. If you take the words literally, the phrase is "long-winged nostril" in the original language. The nostril part undoubtedly connotes a snort, perhaps even the increased respiration of one who is stressed. We tell people to take a deep breath when they're angry, knowing intuitively that they'd benefit by breathing themselves back to a better state. The long-winged element of the Hebrew phrase puts in mind a soaring bird, with a vantage point above the immediacy of getting one's way or not. There's always been peace in the longer view, with seeing where things are headed. Getting angry happens because somebody clipped your wings, and when you landed, helplessly on the ground, they started choking you out. Disempowered, panting, thwarted. I take comfort in that I cannot choke out the Creator with my hands. God is long-winged in the nostril; God has the kind of perspective and disposition where panting like a victim without options isn't possible.

Jesus said if you've seen me you've seen the Father. Someone else said later that Christ is an exact stamp of what God is. And this Christ didn't go around getting things done with intimidation. Sure, fear is often the beginning of wisdom, but as a measure of our initial ignorance. Being afraid of electricity and venomous spiders is an important place to start. But you trade fear for understanding and awareness. You come to enjoy a non-anxious awe. Staying *afraid* is probably a strong sign that I am remaining ignorant. Electricity is a great example for me: I won't replace a switch in my bathroom wall because I don't know electricity. I've heard if I don't engage electricity the right way, it'll hurt me. Even kill me. So I avoid it.

Christ told people not to be intimidated. "Do not be afraid." Get past that beginning phase of ignorance and wake up. Probably because he knew that if you are worried that your behavior could spoil the Cosmic mood, you'll hide. You'll pretend. You'll become fake.

All hiding and lying are rooted in fear. Why would Truth incentivize us to fear, knowing what we will do with it? You'll never have the peace people of faith are supposed to have if you live afraid of the one who cannot help but Love you. You will lie. You will avoid. And even if you call the way you hide your inner world in order to look comparatively blameless "holiness," it's still an awful, nervous lie. If this is what the God of eternity wants from us, you and I are in big trouble forever. There's no way to be at peace with ourselves and with our Creator if we can make each other and God mad.

A man tells his new bride he'll be ten minutes late. She huffs in aggravation, her mood souring, teaching him over time that his punctuality is the knob controlling her joy.

Toward the end of the quarter the manager becomes a

relational minefield when numbers are low. The performance of the team doesn't just affect revenue, but actually controls their manager's mood, which directly affects the office atmosphere.

A kid tells his parents that his grades are slipping and asks for help. Rather than a supportive response for help and understanding, disappointment fogs the room and the grades prove to be as much about his value as his studies.

In each case, people discover that someone becomes unsafe when they're exposed to reality. Those who act out have the same problem Jack Nicholson accuses Tom Cruise of having in *A Few Good Men*—they can't handle the truth! And so people are motivated to protect both themselves and the other from the whole story, because moody beings tend to have little capacity for what's true. If I got a nickel for every time this dynamic was at play in the couples I counsel, this book could be printed on gold leaf and not set me back at all.

The man calls his wife and says he'll be home in five minutes. He knows he's twenty minutes away, but he'll just blame traffic or something later, because pacifying her with lies, even though it's wrong, seems best.

The sales team pads their numbers, makes up sales call logs, exaggerates performance. The truth might come out later, but for now they pacify with lies and keep the easily overwhelmed beast asleep.

The child did everything in his understanding to improve his grades, but to no avail. So he blames a surprise test, his mean teacher. Then he figures out an F can be transformed into a B with no artistic effort at all. Since happiness and acceptance are conditional on good grades, not what's actually true, he lies. He's wrong to, but who willingly tanks others' moods when they learn life can at least *seem* better with a little fiction? The boy grows up to be a moody manager who calls his wife on his way home with intentionally bad ETAs, and comes to feel a little bifurcated inside when he thinks about how angry God might be if God ever looked and listened to his life more closely.

Some aren't willing to lie. But they are willing to avoid you or not tell you anything at all. Same motivator. When someone's mood proves to be circumstantial, his or her joy conditional, nobody wants to mess with those circumstances and conditions. If you show that your happiness and approval are dependent on specific outcomes and performances, you will often be lied to, sometimes avoided, and sometimes deliberately left out of the loop "for your own protection."

Let's face it: if you're moody, anxious, and easily rattled by the universe not being what you want, the people around you are probably deceiving you in some measure. If you can't handle a thing, people won't hand it to you.

Paul listed nine words that reflect tangible evidence that the Spirit, rather than the tick, is influencing our behavior:

Love.

Joy.

Peace.

Patience.

Kindness.

Goodness.

Faithfulness.

Gentleness.

And . . .

Self-control.

Again, these words are about what we provide to the experience of others. The arrows turned more away than toward the self. Light spreading from the bulb and filling a room. The evidence of the Spirit's sway in my life begins with Love of others and ends, for Paul, with me controlling me. Not me controlling you and you controlling me. Not circumstances controlling me. Not the weather, not the outcome of the election, not even the final score of the game. Frankly, not even God, despite the loftiness of the request that God take me over. The fruit of the Spirit isn't the control of the Spirit. Wanna see evidence on my life that I'm following Christ in human adulthood: I master myself and leave you out of that responsibility.

My refusal to allow anyone power over what I am or how I feel is an act of courageous and inspired Compassion. I take back from you the ability to shape my mood. I withdraw from you my blame, my fault-finding, my decision to enjoy my life.

I control me. You're welcome.

There are days when I wish the fruit of the Spirit *was* that I got to control other people, or control circumstances to conform them to my liking. And there are just as many days when I wish the fruit of the Spirit was an inspired ability to persuasively assign blame to all those responsible for my soured disposition and lack of happiness.

And yet there's a real sense of power that comes from knowing Christ wants to teach me the Compassion and the strength in not being so subject to the (mis)behavior and (s)words of others. To take back the remote and responsibility for the enjoyment of my own life.

This self-control is a beautiful display of the best kind of Power. Power that God has and gives. Power that soars high above and sees and blesses, and isn't given to tantrums because it disallows anyone else to futz with the remote.

14

→

The strangely transformative effect of letting people be

A THIRD SET OF LIGHTS and sirens passed a few hundred yards behind our house and, rather than fading into the distance, stopped. Close. Dad muted the *M*A*S*H* rerun and pushed away his spaghetti-topped TV tray. He craned his neck to see through the window. "What in Sam Hill?" I still don't know what this phrase means.

A sheriff's deputy had raced to the dam at our end of the lake, meeting the other deputies already parked. They cut their sirens, but their lights still had the fall trees strobing Americana. Something big was going down. Big enough for Dad to finally turn the TV off on Margaret "Hot Lips" Houlihan.

"Dad, where are you going?" I asked in a way that seemed masculine to me, a halo of spaghetti sauce and a dozen downy hairs on my fourteen-year-old lip.

"I'll be right back, stay here."

My dad had been a cop since before I was born. It was his

nature to involve himself in such matters. My brother and I, barely teenagers, watched through the windows as my dad became a small, shimmery silhouette down by the deputies' cars at the lake.

After twenty minutes he came back through the sliding glass door. He went to his bedroom, to the closet where his uniform and holster hung. As he moved, he explained what had happened.

A man had made a surprise visit to his girlfriend's house to confront her about her cheating ways. He'd come in to find her with the very man he'd suspected her of straying with. Suspicions confirmed, enraged screaming ensued. She implored him to calm down. "We're just talking, it's not what it looks like." All that. The man was persuaded otherwise, produced a gun, and shot the home-wrecker right where he sat on the couch.

Dead.

The woman shrieked as the cuckold ran. And he had run to our lake neighborhood, and was now feared to be trying to gain entrance into one of the few houses on our end of the lake. Our house was as good a candidate as any. Somewhere in this story my young eyes came out of their sockets.

My dad pulled his service revolver, a .357, from its holster. My brother and I were being given curt instructions. Dad was in some mode, dispensing facts without feeling. He laid another gun on the bed. A snub-nosed .38 Special. One of those guns TV cops strap to their ankles just in case the last scene calls for it. I remember it looking small but being cratered by the comforter because of its weight. This gun was assigned to me.

"Stay here, keep the doors locked, and stay away from the

windows." I wasn't to touch the gun unless necessary. Many fathers give the birds-and-bees talk to their young sons. My dad deputized me.

Dad slipped out into the dark on a manhunt. I stayed with my brother, pacing from one end of the house to the other, wondering and shuddering. An hour or so passed before my brother and I heard a gunshot echoing across the lake and ricocheting like a weak cough through naked trees and dry air. Dad returned and explained to us the man had swum far out into the frigid water my brother and I played and fished in, put his gun in his mouth, and pulled the trigger. A murder-suicide had just happened in our sleepy little neighborhood.

Later that evening I guess we just went to bed. No one felt good about what had happened, and yet our own consciences could rest easy that in this tragedy we were the good guys, the defenders and enforcers, powerful and true.

I never wanted to be a cop as far as I can recall. But I loved the kind of power that came with such a career. My dad was the one dad who caused my friends to fall silent when he came into the room. I called my friends' dads by their first names. But my friends wouldn't look my dad in the eye. My dad had a badge. My dad held the power of the State of Ohio. My dad carried life and death on his hip and made less-scrupled folks' palms sweat when he drove behind them. There was the law and his enforcement of it. He was to me a representative of an absolute law. He was an agent of conformity to this absolute law. My dad was the government.

We learn power, and the assurances having this power provides, from our father figures. This is the man from whom I learned it. I learned it by observation. And I learned it by engaging with his sharp, commonsense, right-side-of-the-issues mind.

At one point I became a pastor. We all want to honor our fathers, and sometimes the best way to honor someone is to expand on their idea. So where Dad donned a badge and gun, I wielded a Bible. He had the state behind his work. I was sanctioned by the Kingdom of Heaven. I loved the idea—despite my inability to see and admit it in the beginning—that I could speak words into a microphone and others felt goaded to change their life's path. I carried life and death, translated into readable English with notes and maps, on my hip, and made less-scrupled

folks' palms sweat when I drove my interpretations into them. There was God's law, and my enforcement of it. I was a representative of an absolute law. An ordained agent of conformity to this absolute law. My dad's son was a church leader.

Control of others, attempted and justified with select Bible verses, was intoxicating. Especially when it was in harsh judgment of situations like someone actually getting intoxicated. To change people into something more in keeping with my preferences was the exact expression of power I desired, and it could be called The Lord's Work, to boot. I not only conformed myself to this code, but was deputized by Officer Jesus to get others to be like me. Or else.

I remember my stepmother, who had seen me go through various juvenile phases of trying to find the thing that made me feel important, asking about my newfound faith and the instant leadership and influence that came with it. She said, "It must feel good to have something so significant to be a part of." She was trying to affirm me. To be kind. I took it as an open door through which to run and start making pronouncements: "What feels good about it, Sandy, is knowing I'm right." I was hoping she'd push back with something relativistic or progressive so I could assault her with John 14 or my rudimentary attempts at thrashing postmodernism. She stared, smiling. She recognized a narrow-skulled zealot when she saw one, though she had the grace not to say anything, waiting still for me to grow up. But *she* could give this grace to me from houses away. My own wife had to suffer daily from my lusty grasp on the power of Christian monochromatic, patriarchal, unthoughtful absolutism.

It was almost too good to be true that the Bible had verses in it that I could read as permission—as *duty* even—to put her under my tutelage and reign. As it has been for many child men, my being dubbed Spiritual Head of Household without vetting of character or measuring of wisdom was a can of worms that disgusted more than it caught any fish. I remember numerous arguments with Kristi where she said my sudden role as Spiritual Leader was more a case of Spiritual Enforcer. It's an ironic observation to look back on, recognizing how much I was actually trying to turn the pastorate into a Fraternal Order of Police. Thank God for a wife who put up with exactly 0 percent of my juvenile zealotry.

It's hard (impossible?) to be compassionate when what is valued most is controlling and converting and subduing. But it's tricky to recognize this, since it feels to the controller like a necessary, even welcomed, act. *I know what's best, and so it is from my love that I take away your autonomy and disregard your human dignity. You'll thank me later.* But true Compassion is the suspension of power and control and command as we usually think of them, so that the interests of others can be put first. Not what their interests *should* be. But real, ungoverned acceptance and recognition. It's that susceptible, uncomfortable place that says, through gnashed teeth, *Despite my impulse to make sure my will has prominence, in the face of my desire to have control and to have you conform to my way rather than the other way around, I concede. Because, as I think about it, my priorities becoming yours is what I want, so I will give this very thing to you.*

If Compassion isn't our inspiration here, then at least let us be reminded that Jesus warned that when we throw our pearls to pigs—animals his first audience had determined were too beneath righteousness to even be included in the food chain—we get what is precious to us trampled and ourselves bitten. Control says, "I was only trying to help." Compassion says, "Who do I think I am, judging you to be a pig in need of my pearls? Sorry about that, please forgive my intrusion."

Learning Compassion for others requires my being released from an addiction to a childish understanding of power as well as from my invalidated lust to conform others to my will. This requires me to recognize over and over, perhaps with daily reflection and prayer, that I am invited to follow not so much a caricature of an "Almighty God"—the sky king with all the winning arguments and missiles to defend them—but a vulnerable Rescuer who willingly condescended to such an extent that it looked like loss by the time the Romans were finished with him. This is true, matured power apparently: the suspension of the pursuit of almightiness for the sake of the other. It takes faith.

Maybe it *is* faith. The cop, the church leader, the human being duped into a silly understanding of power, releasing the illusion of control, deferring to the other despite the internal insistence that *I'm right and you're wrong and I can prove it.* It's not been intuitive for someone raised on the power curriculum I was raised on, but I am increasingly convinced that I am never less loving of you than when I am trying to control you, trying to reshape you into something more in keeping with my supergreat collection of ideas. In fact, it's clear to me that that's me loving me, disguised poorly as me loving you.

There are few better tells that my inner world has gone unfaced and left unseen by the light of Truth than when I start trying to control the exterior world with, ultimately, juvenile understandings of power.

But with this desire to overpower recognized and suspended to the degree it's seen, what's left? I suppose I am left loving you just as you are. I suppose I am left with only my observable life as my authoritative statement on what I think is best. My life as my embodied advertisement for what I believe to be best. My day-to-day existence as the enforcement of the Kingdom in which I hope; my way as my declaration of what's right and beautiful and good. And unless you ask me to get involved, or are oppressed by others whose idea of power is as delusional and toxic as mine used to be, I simply take you as you present you.

Convert me, Love you.

My well-intended ego prefers to reverse those values to Love me, Convert you, so I have to work this out each morning with fear and trembling.

Over the years some folks have thought me to be a deficient

Evangelical according to their expectation that my message and methods should be heavily focused on conversion. The more I learn about Love and fear, the less I want to make anybody be any different than they are. I don't imply those who more directly associate with the label "Evangelical" automatically make the mistake of Loving people less. I merely offer a caution by way of my own experience: If conversion is part of your spiritual identity, whatever the religious or denominational label, the stage is set for exactly this mistake. Loving someone while also believing you're responsible for getting them to become other than who they are—which generally means the convertee is expected to become more like the convertor—has too often made brother and sister into salesman and client. Cop and criminal.

Convert yourself, Love others, and watch the world heal. This is a high, confident view of the power of Love and the conviction that what's true, rather than what's forcibly pretended, will save us.

The first woman saw an old house, deteriorated and neglected, and began to dream of fully restoring it to its intended condition.

The second woman looked at an old house, curled her nose, and took to sketching out her dream home.

The first sought to understand the original architecture, the period's wood and stone, the history of the property, and those who had used the house before.

The second comparison-priced general contractors, then went shopping for paint colors, sofas, and interior design magazines.

The first worked tirelessly, patiently restoring the interior and exterior of the house in perfect accord with its former self.

The second changed and updated every interior and exterior surface, painting and modernizing in perfect accord with her tastes and the latest trends.

The first was thrilled to see the house returning to itself after so many years.

The second was thrilled to see her plans becoming a reality.

The first woman, after a great many months, made the house everything it was meant to be.

The second woman soon made the house everything she'd always wanted.

Both women's hearts were good.

But only the first house felt loved.

15

→

God Loves you*

*the right-now you, not potential you

JESUS WAS GETTING READY to make something of an inaugural
address. He'd be done in less than twenty minutes, if the number
of words we have recorded are any indicator. It would come to be
known as the Sermon on the Mount.

As a pro tip to preachers, a full read-through of this sermon
clocks in at under twenty minutes at a comfortable, Midwest-
erner's pace. Let us take note. Or, rather, let us take less notes.

By any standard, it was a good sermon. But the congregation
hearing this sermon was a disaster.

The sermon begins in Matthew chapter 5. At the end of
chapter 4 we get a who's who of those in attendance. There are
Jews from Judea, Jerusalem, and Galilee. Adjusting for the glaring
absence of a middle class, this means there were potentially scores
of farmers, fishermen, and masons, a sea of blue collars, gathered
with the religious elite from the holy city. Those elite would have
representatives from the Pharisees—a Hebrew term that means

"separatist." These were the traditionalists who knew who was pure, who was impure, and what needed to be done about this filthy world. The Sadducees, in many respects opposed to the Pharisees, were the majority group. These were the scriptural literalists, demanding people just do what their favorite part of the Bible said and stop believing everything else because nothing else was binding. Also present were those from the Decapolis, the ten cities. This collection of city-states had very little in the way of a Semitic population and would have brought a little Roman, pagan flavor to the mix Jesus was addressing. Reasonably speaking, this was the Sermon to the Mixed Bag.

Present also were newly healed paralytics, wondering what they were going to do for cash now that they couldn't legitimately beg.

There were also recently healed epileptics, thankful and stepping cautiously in their conditioned anticipation of their next violent episode.

And there were freshly exorcised demoniacs, having to themselves their own mind and will and desires for the first time in forever. These guys probably had the best stories.

This crowd is referred to, interestingly, as the *crowds*. Some translations render it *multitudes*. It's an unnecessary plural when you think about it. Why pluralize a plural unless you want to communicate that the crowd didn't think of themselves as one big group, but several? Pockets of differently valued and valuing people. The know-it-alls and the critics and the healing and the forgotten and the callous-handed and the hopeful and the barely interested, all in their little clusters, forming one checkered mass on the hillside.

Jesus sat down on this hillside in the midst of this collection of collections, cleared his throat, and spoke. We've long heard the Beatitudes as a stiff list of *blesseds*. This word can reasonably be translated "happy," which might give some new dimension to some familiar words:

Happy in their Spirits are the very ones you think
should be sad. The poor.
They're the possessors of the Empire of God!

Happy are those who mourn for better days. They'll get them.

Happy are those who don't try to muscle their way
into everything. They're already written into the will.

Happy are those who are starved for more than just dinner,
but long for things to be as they should be.
That meal will soon be served.

Happy are the merciful.
Because what goes around comes around.

Happy are those who've made their hearts pure,
not just their outward behavior. They are the ones who
will see the God the pretenders pretend to know.

Happy are the ones who make and keep peace.
They, not the ones who attack others in God's name,
are the children of God.

Happy are the ones persecuted for making things better,
because they are establishing residence
in the Kingdom of Heaven.

Happy are the ones slandered and troubled by others
for associating with what I'm about. They're in good company,
because the prophets of God have always had tough lives
and we always celebrate them for it later.

This was a confusing way to start a sermon. It seemed clear that Jesus wasn't laying out pathways for obtaining God's Love. He spent his whole ministry deconstructing that ego pyramid. Instead, he seemed to be contradicting social norms. The very people they'd have thought should be dubbed pitiful, pathetic anathema were given the opening lines of the sermon and presented as having what we thought was reserved for a chosen few. "Happy are those you assumed had no reason yet to be happy."

The rich were cocking eyebrows.

The well-educated were waiting for the punchline.

The dregs were scratching their dirty heads, wondering if they'd heard right.

Jesus continued.

"You are the light of the world. You are the salt of the earth. You are a city on a hill."

When he said "you," he used a plural term according to the Greek. His "you" wasn't to any one person. He was saying "y'all." Without qualification, asterisk, or caveat, Jesus just told the whole group of groups—the multitudes—they were the plan. They were collectively light and salt and a city that can't go unnoticed.

The rich over here looking suspiciously at the poor over there. The fishermen gathered over there shrugging hopefully at the plumbers in the back. The religious leaders up front, divided to the right and to the left, wondering who was this "y'all" to whom the Rabbi spoke . . . They'd have to study the Scriptures and argue about words to form their argument.

What a powerful word to say to this group of people in your first sermon. One that must've irritated those who thought of themselves as having earned higher favor, and something that must've staggered those who were literally conceived of as less human for their lack of belongings.

When God called Moses from the burning bush to go free the Israelite slaves, Moses complained that he talked badly and was not good enough at words for speaking.

When God called Gideon to lead, Gideon objected on the grounds that he was a wimp from a family of wusses.

When God called Jeremiah, he explained to God that he couldn't do what was asked because he was just a wittle boy.

Paul was sometimes accused of being a first-century version of the Wizard of Oz: pretty eloquent in his letters, but embarrassingly underwhelming in person. Add to this that he had been complicit in the arrest, murder, and orphaning of Christians before he became one himself.

Over and over, people who self-assess as subpar are told it

won't count against them or their efforts. Over and over, people are told that God won't be using our self-measurement to determine our fitness for participating in good things. But this takes away something our egos cherish: outperforming others, earning what others cannot, obtaining relative advantage. So we ignore Jesus's words and assume the city on the hill is for those of us best suited to build it and be it. The leaders. The loved ones. The lovable ones.

There's a quote on preachers' lips and bumpers and on the internet that represents a certain kind of thinking fairly well. It's a pretty good quote.

God loves you the way you are,
but God loves you too much to leave you that way.

It presents to me an inviting God who approves of the hymn "Just as I Am" but who also has in mind to address my desperate need for overhaul. There's enough warmth and truth in this for me to respect it. But there's another angle in it to consider as I learn Compassion is antithetical to control.

Christ summarized faith as Love of other. It all hangs on Compassion for the other just as we want Compassion for ourselves. On this hang every law and every tradition, according to whom we hold as the Author of it. But many of us have come to believe subtly that the goal is to get right. To change. To surrender to God so that we can be what we were made to be. To make sure we're not just on the hillside, but in the right group in all the groups on the hillside.

How many churches proudly display mission statements

that speak more to the transformation of people than Compassion for them as they are? For some of us, it inspires us forward. Especially around January: *Yes, please, make me a better version of myself than the guy I was stuck with last year.*

For others of us, it's the reason we don't go to church at all. We simply cannot put up with others prodding us to be something they're more comfortable with.

You and I could make a long list of families and friendships that have broken down because faith was understood as the thing that makes you tell people to change. We've conflicted politically, environmentally, morally, relationally, philosophically, theologically, etc., and never once noticed the last four letters of those words. We suffer an inability to embrace difference and to remain unthreatened by the disparate paths of fellow human beings. We childishly think if it's not all one thing, something evil is afoot. But don't you and I wish in our own ways that we could find a place and a people where being loved, being known, and being honest were three strands of the same cord.

To you and me both, and to others around us, Jesus said "y'all."

I spoke with a woman a few years ago who challenged me on what she picked up on as my efforts to morph her into a more palatable being for myself. Someone formed in my own image. A clone, rather than a sister.

She asked me questions that were extremely disruptive. Especially in that the questions birthed more questions in my mind rather than answers. I wrote down these questions in my journal and they went something like this:

If God's ultimate goal is to change me, isn't this saying God has chiefly in mind to make me into someone else, which means

God Loves what I might become but is less into me now? If God Loves me, why change me? I have never changed a thing I made that I said I Loved just as it was.

My wife never feels loved when I tell her she has to change or behave differently for me to fully accept her. How can you accept a thing you want to change?

Is this all a really sneaky way of saying God actually Loves everyone to different degrees, based on how much they've come to conform with God's preferences? And, therefore, isn't God's Love as finicky, metered, and conditional as mine?

And what if I don't want to be like the people God allegedly approves of more? What if what's presented as "surrendered to God's will" and therefore "more in divine alignment" is repulsive or obnoxious to me? This isn't hypothetical. Some people who become followers become more in need of adjustment after their conversion than before. I know this firsthand; I see a life-sized picture of one of these twits above my bathroom sink every morning.

Jesus's public ministry began on a hillside and was staggeringly, insultingly inclusive and gracious.

And the end of his public ministry, found at the very end of the Gospel of Matthew, is the same:

> The eleven disciples went to Galilee, to the mountain Jesus told them to go to. When they saw him, alive and well, they fell down and worshiped him. *But some of them doubted.* And Jesus approached and said to *them,* "All heavenly and earthly authority has been given to me. So go, make students of all nations, immersing them

into the united reputation and character of the Father, the Son, and the Holy Spirit, teaching them to live by all I have commanded you to live by. And know that I am always with you, always."

Worshipers and doubters. Arms raised and arms folded. Blessed assurance alongside, *Well, I've been reading Bart Ehrman, so I'm not so sure . . .*

To "them" he spoke. "Them" without distinction. Y'all. Because Compassion for people as they are was, for the faith elite, one of Jesus's most aggravating idiosyncrasies. Despite our familiarity with—and our *preference* for—Love being more rooted in what we get right, true Love and Compassion are actually something else. A prerequisite for change that is *called* Love is something many of us avoided as soon as we had the ability to choose not to go to church anymore, because our hungry souls couldn't survive on such carrot-and-stick transactions. It's not that we didn't want Love and Faith and God. We just didn't want to find out Jesus picked people to Love like that popular kid chose kickball teams.

We all want to transform into the best version of ourselves. Perhaps what slowly changes us in the most meaningful ways is learning that, even if we don't change, we are as Loved as anyone ever was. Maybe the peace that comes from recognizing I don't have to behave desperately anymore is what changes me, rather than rules telling me to "stop it or else." Maybe that insatiable hunger for acceptance and validation is satisfied when I understand that my performance and achievements don't buy me Love or inclusion. I am Loved because I exist, and therefore there's nothing to extract or persuade or steal. Maybe seeing myself in light of unconditional inclusion helps me to stop settling for superficial responses to my appetites. Maybe I stop believing that all I am is a bundle of appetites that need to be addressed, and I begin risking the joy of connection as I already am. Maybe I'm enough now—before I, others, or even religion begins meddling. Maybe acceptance is the best meddling.

What we call sin—which in a faith summarized by the Love of other must be defined by the withholding of Love—is remedied by our decreasing desire to use and abuse others. To Love rather than extract love. Use and abuse wane as we come to trust that we already have all we need, and already are what we're trying to become: lovable. A lot of childish, foolish, sinful, toxic insanity has fallen off of me in the light of others' Compassion toward me. So of course I'm moved to share Compassion with others. What else can a reflective surface do with Light but share it? By this, I suppose, I am not such a deficient evangelist after all. So I bring good tidings of great news that I hope you'll pass on to the multitudes:

Y'all are as Loved in this moment as y'all could ever be. And however bewilderingly, y'all are already the hands and feet of this Love. And I keep repeating it because as it sinks in, we become capable of this very same Love toward others. And the world heals.

16

→

If "stop it" worked,
Jesus coulda stayed home

JESUS SOUNDS LIKE HE'S GOT A megaphone to his lips outside a rock concert in the opener to Mark's gospel. He was talking repentance, that thing where people undergo dramatic changes— removing piercings and tossing out albums and never again wishing others a limp and secular "Happy Holidays" in December— and where maybe what I said in the last chapter is wrong.

> *The time is complete, and the kingdom of God is at hand;*
> *repent and believe the good news.*
> —Jesus, Mark 1:15, my rendering

The word *repent* has come to look best in picket sign scrawl. Few words have as much baggage. I've heard it shouted by one sinner at another quite a few times, which reminds me the worst sins are always other people's.

I used to imagine Jesus shouting down sinners this same way. The one big difference being he did so from a perfect life. But then I started to notice that in the Bible religious folks told him to repent and even called him a devil, so perhaps his repent was different from theirs.

The word, at least originally, has more to it than behavior modification. Translated from the Greek, it literally means "change your thinking" or, as we might say today, "Wake up!" It's less a demand that others stop doing something and more the chime of a soul's alarm clock. You know this intuitively because the checkers in our past generally elicit a "Man, was I an idiot. What was I thinking?" rather than "Man, I am so evil." We know in hindsight most often our issue has been foolishness. A lack of awareness.

There is, according to Christ, a Kingdom in our midst that's over and under and permeating whatever temporal empire or nation or kingdom we may be standing in. Right here, at hand. It's not confined to geography or a yet-to-be-experienced afterlife. It's the state of things being as they are supposed to be. Now. This domain, by Christ's account, is immediately available. Right there in a cubicle, in a ditch where your car's radiator steams, in the penthouse pool cabana, and at the dinner table of our enemies.

Boundless Love.

Infinite resource.

Like treasure buried right in your yard. Thinking differently is the shovel that unearths it. Our being merely good boys and girls may or may not ever have us stumble upon it. In this awakened thinking, we will come to believe some things, to disbelieve some things, to adopt some things, and to let loads and loads of crap go.

An invitation to come awake is very different from a behavioral ultimatum. It's the difference between a nun wielding a ruler and the Christ handing me coffee at my bedside, asking if I'm ready, after all these years, to get out of my bed and live. When we realize demands aren't held over us, then we have a better chance of resisting the urge to hold it over others. As it comes from peace to make peace, repentance is the lifelong process of learning to see goodness, not cease badness. The gift of sight by a Father who doesn't slap hands but washes sleepy eyes. This Kingdom of goodness, we're standing in it. It stands within us. Anywhere, anytime, in anyone, just waiting to be observed. *Repent and see what is.* "The Kingdom of God isn't something you go discover and colonize," Jesus once said. "Nor can anyone legitimately say, 'It's here!' or 'It's there!' Behold, the Kingdom of God is within you."

We spend too much of our lives believing our timid minds. And we use those same timid minds to attempt "repenting" into something that would be observed favorably by God, whom we've really reengineered into a higher-level Santa, if we would dare list out the traits. Our faith is the concerted effort to get him to remove us from the naughty list. This is the cheapest, most played religion.

Repent of this repentance! Leave Santa for the kids.

A god protesting us through angry sign holders in reaction to our sin isn't worth much more than our avoidance. But a God calling us to wake up so we don't get things twisted up in the first place—that's a God who wants to set us up for a win. A God that doesn't try to control our behaviors, but one who teaches us how to control our own minds. To be humans.

History has revealed too many people who have tried
to be spiritual before they have learned how to be human!
It is a major problem. Maybe this is why Jesus came to model
humanity for us—much more than divinity. . . .
Get the ordinary human thing down, and you will have
all the spirituality that you can handle.
—Richard Rohr

I shut off my car in the driveway, and I pause before getting out to go into the house. Why?

Because first I must repent. I must check and likely change my thinking, its content, tone, and frequency. The Kingdom is at hand. Will I see it, or will I go into my house and encounter my family believing my unsophisticated, unadjusted selfishness?

I'm heading into a meeting. First, I should go repent in the restroom. There, in a stall designed to shield others' eyes as I dis-pose of that which has no value to me, I ask myself if I'm feeling ripped off by anyone or anything, recently or ever. Do I feel generally owed? I try to walk out of that place, my hands washed, my eyes open to how paid in full I may choose to be at any moment, and therefore how uninhibited I can be in Loving like I like to be Loved.

In a few moments I am going to ask my children to explain why, other than the fact that they are children, they haven't done what they've been told to do. I must repent first: Have unmet expectations, condescension, humiliation happened to me today, motivating me to demand the members of my household give me what I've been robbed of? Am I going to be my children's loving father or a bullying, wounded ego? Will I teach them "power" or strength? Will they walk away feeling Loved or fought? Once I repent, I may not even need to bring up their youthful oversight. Funny thing about getting logs out of my eye first; I often find there was no speck in your eye in the first place.

I'm having a conversation and I feel the urge to start talking. Perhaps the urge to begin out-storytelling you. I repent. Can't I just listen to someone else's good or terrible day and leave myself out of it unless invited? *Wake up, Steve, or you'll sleepwalk all over them.*

Before I go into school, or work, or into a conversation, or before I think about commenting online, I must remember to repent. This way I don't unthinkingly believe people must approve of me for me to have value. That people must be sexually attracted to me for me to have a sense of worth. That my witty criticisms on government, an opposing team, the board of directors, or the manufacturers of a product will somehow translate into my being seen as intelligent, boosting my social rank. I must evaluate what I think are pearls, whom I'm calling pigs, and what Love demands I do if I'll repent enough to hear the instructions. I must repent in my mind over and over or I'll default to a kingdom of Me. The Kingdom, whose economy is Compassion and not morality, is right there, roaring like a spring under my feet. I just have to remember the importance of dowsing for it. I have been gifted the control of my mind, if only

I'll care enough to remember I have it. When we see our minds are an engine waiting to be fired up, *repent* isn't "stop it" as much as it is "start it." It's about finally beginning. Sanely. Lovingly. Awake and aware.

The Kingdom is at hand. For the Love of God, don't sleep through it.

17

Speed trap

My wife and I debated recently about police and the role they play in enforcing the law. My wife was commonsensical about it. Yet we were debating. That's probably enough information for you to determine which of the two of us was being reasonable.

I admitted to her my argument was likely fueled by some Officer Daddy issues for me. Still, I spoke with frustration about how the human ego, plus power, never works out 100 percent great for the people under that power. I argued cops are necessary and mostly good, but when they're bad it's so bad.

Kristi agreed that there are flaws in the system(s), even severe flaws, but that the alternative scenario I was implying was far from realistic.

I spoke of my specific irritation that a traffic officer can decide to give you a ticket or not, based on his or her mood, let alone realities such as racial bias. I'd had officers tell me it was my lucky day, that *they liked me*. I argued that this was an example of them having way too much discretion for something dubbed law enforcement. Either take away this fickle judiciousness or put chips in our car that record our speed and send us a monthly bill for speed overages. I didn't fully believe this simple binary solution, but I needed something to bolster my position since she had common sense on her side.

"But if the speed limit is fifty-five," she said, "and you are going fifty-seven, you are breaking the law. Plain and simple. You agreed to the terms when you got a license, and agreed again when you got on the road with the signs that present to you the speed *limit*"—she emphasized that the word on the sign is *limit*—"so you should accept that you are breaking the law and that there are consequences. If an officer decides instead of ticketing you to warn you, in the spirit of goodwill, then that is a gift. But the fact remains: *you* are the one breaking the letter of the law. Not the officer. It's not perfect, but it works."

I struck back with something that sounded really philosophical. "My basic point is that moral people don't need laws and immoral people don't obey them. It doesn't work well enough."

"But it works better than doing nothing," Kristi insisted. "Being pulled over, the very threat of it, keeps selfish idiots from assigning to themselves their own speed limit. Think of the people who would be dead if not for the system applied, flawed as it is."

The next day I thought about how, to a ridiculous degree, the issue wasn't the way the law is applied. It was that I don't like being forced to submit to it. It was that I don't want to be told what to do, especially if this enforcement comes at the discretion of another human being. I call my own shots, partner.

The issue, when I experimented with some honesty—which I'd not well attempted during my conversation with my wife—was that I want to be regarded as *special*. Exceptional. Not subject to the same structures and guidelines as others. You see, I'm a great driver. Not just in the typical "I'm above average because I'm an American" way. I'm saying I actually scored 100s on both my driving tests and memorized every second of the car chase from *The French Connection*. I'm a real peach and want to be revered.

This wasn't really about driving. It was about me, the proverbial man in the rearview mirror, and what psychologists call the Self-Serving Bias: a penchant we have for favorably excusing ourselves from the average or the whole. The law isn't necessary for me and my framework, but you need it. I am capable of tremendous superiority, and the only reason I don't achieve it is because of everyone else.

A friend of mine sent me an email the next day. He had no idea about the debate I'd had with my lower-test-score-achieving spouse. Totally unsolicited but apparently prompted by the one who sided with my wife, my friend had copied and pasted some thoughts he'd written down during Lent a couple years back and sent them to me to see what I thought.

One section said, "I had to start thinking about all the things I do that are not loving. All the things I do that get in the way of love. Like speeding. That just popped in my head as I drove. How does speeding affect my ability to love? Because I am more impatient with those around me when I speed. I do little things like rush yellow lights and tailgate those who are not in the same hurry."

But then he posited the negative side effects of being a slower, more responsible driver. That it wasn't the speed so much as his attitude at the wheel:

"I could start judging all those reckless drivers who are insisting on going over the speed limit. Or create an inconvenience of slowing someone down in a hurry . . ." My friend seemed to understand what my ego didn't want to understand. The problem comes from thinking I'm something superior to what all us drivers are: *traffic*.

My desire to see myself as special, to be seen by others as exemplary, cuts me off from the "we" and makes me a disruptive problem for the whole. Speeding in traffic because I'm a better driver than you, or slowing down because I'm a more sane driver than you—both have a way of dislodging me from you. I become the center and you are *othered*. Validation for what we achieve is perfectly fine, and we all like to hear from others that we can do great things. But we have to be cautious with how we calibrate this desire for specialness, because it can cause problems in the same way that one special cell that does its own thing is called cancer and is lethal to the whole. If I'm exempt, I probably demand more consideration than I give.

And I'll even argue with my wife not so much on the merits of the points she is making, but for the lost ground my remarkable self is suffering. *If you're right, then I have to be equal. How can I hoard extra cans of nonperishable Love in the nervous bunker of my personality if I'm no more special than anyone else?*

Paul gambled a bit by adding the term *self-control* to his list of relationship features notable in someone living by the Spirit of Christ. The ego can easily read it and feel vindicated in its oppositional "no one tells me what to do" MO. My ego is always looking for the exemption. A way of submitting you to things I shouldn't be expected to submit to. Community immunity. Present, special, and yet somehow hovering above it all. Tony Stark without the genius or cash. My ego speaks loud and clear:

I'm not interested in your story, because it's not interesting.
Listen to mine.

I'm not going to recycle. Others can, but I don't have time
for that BS and I do enough other good stuff.

I'm not going to put money in the honor system cup because
I'm otherwise honorable. Enough others already did anyway.
But you better chip in, thief!

I'm not going to sit all the way through this presentation.
I'll get up and refill my drink and go pee.
But if you guys go too, that's rude.

I believe in forgiveness, but I'm not going to forgive her.
That girl was rude, and no one treats me that way.

I'm late because my morning was crazy and traffic
was ridiculous. You're late because you're irresponsible.

Once I taught Kenyan church leaders in a dung hut for four hours. We talked about unity and creative ways to unite those who have gotten too good at living in response to what makes them different. Then we took communion together, all the different denominations and backgrounds, under one roof, at one table. It was beautiful.

At the same time there was a medical team treating everything from headaches to the deleterious effects of AIDS. Women and children had waited in line since before dawn to be seen by a member of our team, who was the only doctor they'd encountered in years.

When I was done with my presentation, and our time of communion had come to an end, one Kenyan pastor shook my hand and thanked me. He then walked out into the midday sun and cut to the front of the one-hundred-yard-long line of people waiting to see the doctor.

"Brother?" I said as I walked up to him. I tried not to sound indignant, but I was genuinely astonished. "What are you doing? Shouldn't you and I go to the back of the line since we came last, and especially since we are trying to put the Love of others on display for this divided community?" I was probably out of line here, having little context in that moment and being capable of great self-exemptions in my own continent. But, hey, I'm a better-than-average driver. "Aren't you showing others that somehow you are to be favored for your position in the church?"

"Ah, yes. But you see," he explained in his delightful accent, thumbing toward people behind him who held motionless infants, whose bodies were stuck in yearlong stoops, who were holding dirty cloths to unhealed lesions. "I am not sick. I am *ill.*" He went on to explain his take on the difference between these two terms, and that he had a throb in his chest he really wanted to have checked out.

This is what he was basically saying to me: *I am special. And my needs are the priority; why else would my feelings be so strong about them? Others are subject to processes and protocol. I am exempt.*

There was a bit of a throb in my chest too, knowing we still had the Lord's Supper in our teeth and yet we were both so acutely capable of self-prioritization and communal exemption, even at the expense of those we live with.

There's no scenario outside of literal death where the ego is eradicated. The sense of self and its protection are part of the human experience. Which means to deny it makes you either a liar or an alien. Turning the dial to at least "51 Percent Others" every day, multiple times a day, and then remaining aware of all the ways we try to subvert this setting in favor of the self, is what it means to have a repentant, awakened mind.

But an awakened mind is risky. When we open ourselves to communion with other and with the Spirit of Love, we make ourselves vulnerable. What happens when we are sick/ill but are so sober in self-assessment that we take the 101st spot in line for the doctor? It could be dangerous. Yet somehow, also, inspiring. Like a perfect man being impaled on a tree for the good of those who may do little more than turn his words into an income.

The ego wants VIP status. It can barely understand the point of living without it. May I be the thunderstorm, but never a raindrop. It drones on and on: *I am superior or I am nothing. I am special, notice me—my value depends on being especially noticed. I resent those who get noticed more. Like me. My circumstances excuse me from the whole.*

Convincing the ego—a term Saint Paul was probably getting at when he spoke of the "flesh"—to be subdued by what's better for the many will require inspiration. Love awakens and reawakens, moment to moment, by reminding us of the life of Jesus and then whispering a reminder about the Golden Rule. Silly as it seems, we already know this so well we made a bracelet out of it: *What Would Jesus Do?* Because we already know what the ego wants to do, and the fallout that can happen if we concede to it. And so we study his life and listen for the whisper until we find ourselves seeing that Compassion for the other is of higher value than a life of self-interest. "You were called to freedom, brothers and sisters," Paul said to his Galatian family. "Just don't turn your freedom into an opportunity for the ego. Instead, through love, serve one another. Because the entire Law of God is fulfilled in this sentence: 'You shall love your neighbor as yourself.'" It's hard. Like I said, it'll take some inspiration and gentle reminders. And be prepared, this is all made even more difficult when you prioritize another out of your conviction that behaving in such a recalibrated way is better for all, but the other is still clawing through life the old uncalibrated way. It will feel like you put your last coin in the slot, but the bag of chips only managed to get lodged against the glass. What a rip-off. How Jesus must have sighed at feeding the five thousand when a thousand of them probably felt they had a meal coming and another hundred complained the fish was cold. But he served them anyway, and Love won the day.

It is well to remember that the entire universe,
with one trifling exception, is composed of others.
—John Holmes

NOTES

PART FIVE

More Than Meets the Eye

Love is not blind—it sees more, not less.
But because it sees more, it is willing to see less.

Rabbi Julius Gordon

18

Her name isn't Mom

THE YEAR IS 3150.

Anthropologists, wearing the reflective silver jumpsuits with chest insignias that all future people wear, are huddled over the opening to a shaft. At the bottom of the shaft lie human bones, old pieces of plastic and glass, and fragments of writings.

Most of the writings are rotted and unintelligible. But one particular section of text is as clear as the day it was printed.

"I have a dream."

This piece of text is preserved and then put on display in the Museum of Histories, Earth/USA Wing. Beneath the sealed text and under soft lighting, where thousands of beings—human and otherwise—can read, is a holographic placard. It says,

The above text, perfectly preserved for over a millennium [Earth years], supports the prevailing theory that Earthlings in this particular hemisphere were enthralled with the science of dreaming.

And then you are unfrozen from your cryogenic slumber. After a few months of stretches and energy shakes, you and some others don silver jumpsuits and go to the museum, where you see the ancient text and the commentary below it. And you come somewhat unglued.

The science of dreaming? What?

The future folks are missing it entirely. Why? Because they don't have context. And without context, they can only go on what they see. They don't understand racism, how it was destroying lives, and how it in many ways came to a head in the 1960s in the strangely segregated southern region of the ironically named United States of America. They are unaware of Dr. King, what he did, said, and why. How great shifts were beginning to take place. What it cost him. How there were frustrating steps forward and back for many decades to come. They do not understand he was hoping aloud in the poetry of an unrealized dream what it would take for the quality of the human experience, irrespective of one's measure of melanin, to increase.

So they just put up a display based on what they *did* know. Intentionally or not, by deciding on the meaning without having the context, they disrespected hundreds of millions of people and Dr. King himself.

⟷

When it comes to history—and even the present, for that matter—there's a lot going on in the past and below the surface that shapes and reshapes how we interpret what we *think* we see and understand. The background always shapes and defines the foreground. That's why when I tell people I have an airbrushed painting of a unicorn hanging on a wall in my home, they look at me with concern. But when I tell them the wall is in my garage, they laugh, somehow relieved. Where it hangs changes its meaning, changes how one receives it and its message.

Searching out and appreciating the not-so-immediately-available context is how we show that we understand—or desire to understand—what's really going on. It's an expression of our sincerity, our taking one another seriously, our Love.

So if Christ's summary of this Book we're trying to take seriously is "Love," then we might need to work on applying the same dutiful contextualizing to the objects of this Love: human beings.

One day my father sat down with me, and we thumbed through an old photo album. Grainy photos of grandparents, great-aunts, and great-uncles I had never met. People dead for so long I didn't even miss them anymore. But my dad started speaking to their context, and to his own.

And tears filled his eyes as he explained the life these photos could only hint about for those who lived outside their context.

His grandfather had committed suicide a few years before I was born. This man was one who made my father feel Loved like almost no other. Made Dad feel like a favorite. But when the old man's wife, my great-grandmother, passed away, followed painfully soon by his daughter, my great-aunt, the man lost his hope and his mind and took his own life in his bathtub with a shotgun.

Soon after that my dad met my mom, and both those teenagers were very quickly thrown into young and unplanned and unprepared parenthood.

And then Dad graduated from the police academy and began dealing with people as a state patrolman, one whom others are rarely glad to see. His job was rewarding, but took an immediate toll. This job he did on swing shifts, for years never finding stability to his rhythm. He enforced the law with a mind bruised from his deceased grandfather, his interactions with the public, and a perpetual lack of sleep.

My mother and father moved half a dozen times, with two young boys in tow, in just a handful of years. Dad was placed and re-placed, as rookies often are. Mom was in many respects a single mother, charged with keeping the peace at home while Dad did it on the roads. Then she had to do it far more diligently when he came home and tried to grab sleep between shifts in the middle of the day, sensitive to every sound inside and outside the house.

In the late seventies, Dad's mother died. He recounted the agony of this as he held the album in his hands, tapping lightly a picture of her holding me in nothing but a diaper. He'd lost his confidant. His advocate. His cheerleader.

Then he lost his father four years later. The only person left to call to ask about electrical work or interest rates, about whether to go this way or that, to remind my dad he was Loved for no reason beyond his existence, was gone. Dad's face seemed younger as he told me all this. Or perhaps Compassion walked me backward in time to see. My father, the barrel-chested cop, turned within half a decade into a twenty-something orphan.

My mother had already lost her father as a teenager. When her father-in-law died, she lost a father again. And she lost some of her husband as well.

Grief and pain descended on my house. Wounded children raising children. There was laughter. I can remember a lot of laughing. But pain and tension undergirded it. My young mind had been oblivious.

After a few more years, Mom and Dad lost their marriage to each other. Things like finances and communication always get top billing for divorce's cause, but I think unaddressed trauma is what took down my home.

One house became two. Christmas got complicated. Birthdays became unrecognized competitions. Easy things became hard. Hard things went unattended. The simple act of my parents writing down their child's home address on school forms became a reminder and an emotional provocation. Honoring their sons' other parent, who was their ex, who was moving on with their life at one pace or another, everything was now a balancing act with regret and division for a net. And the original traumas hadn't gone anywhere. Just hidden by being stacked upon.

Dad turned the album's creaky pages, tearfully recounting the chronology. And it occurred to me, like awaking from a coma:

His name isn't Dad.

Her name isn't Mom.

That's just the title a mere *two* people on earth—my brother and I—call them.

He's Jim.

She's Teresa.

There was an entire story, a seemingly infinite amount of context, outside of the framework that I had never seen. There was so much more to him and to her than I had gotten used to interacting with and judging based on it meeting with my preferences and expectations. How hard, how impossible at times, life had been for my parents. "Wait a minute," I later remarked aloud, "they did a helluva job."

Now I was honoring them for who they were outside of my own narrow context. Just like I hope my kids do for me.

I never Loved my parents more as an adult than the day I recognized. And I was never as able to have the Compassion, understanding, acceptance, and the respect that I had when it clicked that they weren't unpaid extras in a movie about me. Now I could see that they were real human beings. If anything, I was the newer cast member in the movie about them. In a strange way, without allowing myself to condescend, this was when my parents became also my brother and sister, because now I could see enough context to suffer with them. Together.

And if Mom and Dad turned out to possess context enough to enhance my value and respect for them to such a staggering degree, who else might not be soulless, nonunion actors in the Steve Show? Who else might have reasons for their beliefs, their actions, their feelings? Who else had backstories for their current performances? Who else might I learn to see?

The word *respect* is made of the words *re* and *see*. It has in it the effort to take another look because the thing is worth more than a first impression. Compassion and Love dictate that we *respect* human beings, over and over and over and over and over and over and over and over, because we're coming to realize our great capacity to totally, embarrassingly misread someone without taking the time to observe the backstory. Yet all we ever wanted was for someone to know ours.

Today, you and I are 99 percent wrong about everyone we hold opinions about. That figure may be low, but I know I'm close. In our growing sense of Compassion, such as we would like leveled at ourselves, let us respect the human beings around us enough to see what lies beneath that which our stubborn, blind minds and made-up thoughts insist they already have pegged.

See. Then re-see. Then re-re-see. Again and again and again, until you know their real name and feel their story like you hope they'll feel yours. Then we will know Love and Compassion and the reason so many stories in the Bible are of Jesus healing eyes.

19

→

Anointing 62 feet

JESUS HAD BEEN INVITED TO DINNER by a man of means. Jesus's disciples, ever his confused entourage, were in tow.

They'd barely finished their appetizers—Caesar salads, no bacon bits—when a woman came in and squatted down at Jesus's feet. This woman, Mary, is presented to us almost completely anonymously save for her name and a wink in the wording that invites us to assume she was a hooker.

The room smelled of veal and bread wine. Words and laughs bounced off the plaster walls. But now the room had fallen silent, overwhelmed with the heavy bouquet of spikenard. This Mary was dumping a jar of the costly stuff all over Jesus's feet.

Messiah, or Greek's *Christ*, translates fairly well to "the oil-anointed one." It's an ancient picture of one having oil applied to their head or body as they become a leader. Inanimate objects are also messiah'ed (oiled) when they become set apart for special use. Mary was doing a few things worth meditating on, but perhaps all four gospel writers capture elements of the scene so we can be a bit aghast at a *woman like this* anointing Jesus as King of the Jews. Imagine a burping contest put on for the Queen of

England. Or "Happy Mother's Day" written with urine in the snow. It's dark comedy to jar the prudent.

"What the heck is she doing?" they asked, now standing. Jesus was still reclined. Notably, Jesus was never as offended as his disciples. Ever.

"That perfume could've been sold and the money given to The Poor," said Judas, who would later sell Jesus and give the money to himself.

"Leave her alone," said Jesus. "This is a beautiful thing. It's an act of worship. It's a very sincere act of devotion, with or without your appreciation of it as such."

"But . . . but . . . but, Jesus, it's three hundred days' wages! What about the poor?" Judas insisted.

"Well, Judas, there will be plenty of poor people for you to serve once I'm out of the way."

As the fragrant puddle under his feet leached across the host's floor, Jesus made a prediction that's held up fairly well: "I tell you the truth, whenever the Good News is told to others, what this woman just did will be part of it. The thing you're accusing her of doing as a fool will actually be memorialized forever!"

There's a church south of my hometown that erected a sixty-two-foot Jesus statue on its property next to the highway. It was rumored to cost between a quarter to half a million dollars. We Christian leaders in town had a field day with that price tag. The crazy thing looked like a million gallons of sculpted Crisco, at a cost that could have instead paid off several low-income homes, fed thousands, all that.

Then I heard one of the leaders of that church explain how often lonely, tired, guilt-laden truck drivers would pull in from off the highway, weeping. That statue's arms seemed to have a magnetic effect for folks who did little but marinate in isolation on their own thoughts. It was a several-story, Semitic-looking lighthouse, offered so that a few ships and their beleaguered captains might not run aground. Turns out, what we had derided as silly waste performed real ministry.

Incidentally, the church I worked at also had a sign out front for passing traffic. We found its dimensions and its cost fully justifiable.

Lightning struck that Jesus statue a few years later. Another condescending field day ensued. "Oh, the irony," we snorted.

The church responded by putting another Jesus in its place. It's still there today, and truck drivers as well as others are still pulling in with gratitude, as I understand it.

There *was* an irony in the lightning strike, when I think about it. But not how I framed it back then. The irony I now see is this: Lightning took down that statue, just as thunderbolt-chucking religion and its adherents try to strike down acts of Compassion because they can't see those acts' value. And yet that statue of Jesus did what Jesus always does: it rose again. Albeit now with a lightning rod poking up from the top of his enormous head. The Alfalfa and the Omega.

Compassion is an astoundingly, frustratingly affirming force. It Loves the other enough to find beauty and meaning in what the rest of us lazily judge as good or bad. *Ahava* Love, the brand that has the other's interests more in view than its own preferences being perfectly tended to, searches and finds the thing to celebrate. Jesus's Compassion for Mary offended his pious-minded followers, but Love recognizes intent and contextualizes others' behavior in the most favorable way it can. "This woman isn't wasting anything. She is showing me an act of Love, because she is pouring out what is dear to her on me. Who cares about it being reasonable or fashionable or understood by anyone but me and her. It's the Golden Rule. It couldn't be more sincere!"

We swoon over clay ashtrays from our children for this same reason. So we have it within us to reframe, to measure more deeply and allow the other's context to tell us what the value of an action is. We have the ability to suspend judgment, criticism, and condemnation because we possess within us a heart of Love that hopes others will assume that we are also, clumsily, ignorantly, doing the very best we know how to do.

What was Mary to do, bring in a fresh perch and a Torah scroll so Judas and Peter wouldn't criticize her? Had she done that, and had that kept the boys quiet, she would have given not from her own heart but from fear's performance. Hands in the air during the praise music like everyone else, hoping no one ever finds out who you really are.

All acts of Love and worship are foolish and misaligned when compared to the one they're aimed at. We're all pouring out sincerely on the feet of a God who remains shrouded in unknowable mystery, all of us hookers trying to approach the Divine in earnest but unaware that what we're offering speaks accurately only in what it speaks of ourselves. It's all a smelly disaster, no one effort more valuable than another. We should get off each other's backs and smile at our efforts, as God must.

To this day I still make fun of those church signs with cheesy puns on them. I'll even snap photos and send them to friends.

Because those are *objectively* bad, see. Like billboards featuring Pistol-Finger Jesus, the sky Caucasian who threatens eastbound traffic. There couldn't actually be any legitimate, sincere, Loving intent in the hearts of the men and women who threw that together, *right?*

20

How to save a galaxy

DARTH VADER, an asthmatic villain for the ages. Everything about him spoke evil to us as kids.

And then George Lucas blew our tiny minds at the very end of the original Star Wars trilogy with the revelation that Darth was less inherently evil, and more temporarily corrupted. Sickened, but now made well by the courageous Love of his own son. *There was good in him all along.* I wouldn't suggest the subsequent prequels merit equal adoration, but learning the young boy who'd become Darth Vader was actually a misdirected, angry child gave more dimension to what was perhaps initially only a flat, wheezing antagonist. Evil is often far more complex, far more responsive to Compassion than we first imagined. Jesus often called people sick, rather than evil, for just this reason.

The Kingdom belongs to children, according to its King. A lot of movies seem to reinforce this truth, often using children's stories to sneak it in. I try to point out these deep themes to my kids after a movie, but as they get older they meet such post-movie devotionals with rolled eyes. So I guess I'll offer them to you:

The Grinch was a scary mountain troll who wanted nothing more sophisticated than to do bad to the good Who people below. But the Grace and Love of one young Who proved he wasn't evil, but marginalized, misunderstood, and subsequently wounded and angry. This Grace and Love enlarged his heart and shrank his petulance, rescuing him.

Despicable Me's Gru is essentially the same villain. A measure of Gru's villainy is his little yellow Minions, who are responsible for product tie-ins ranging from one-eyed yellow Tic Tacs to toilet scrubbers. Is there something we should acknowledge in the fact that these products address both ends of digestion? I digress. Gru comes out on the screen as proudly sinister. And then Love and Compassion show us Gru wasn't evil at all, just temporarily intoxicated by a childish reaction to being rejected and feeling like a constant disappointment. He didn't become good. He discovered he already was.

Megamind is another variation on this theme. The titular villain was the bad to Metro Man's good. And then with time, Love helps him—as well as us in the process—see that he wasn't so much evil as he was unloved, unsupported, and frustrated. He's actually brilliant, though misdirected. Love shows him the good—what Jesus may have called the "immediately available Kingdom of the Heavens"—in him all along.

The list goes on and on, but I fear your eyes may be starting to roll. Suffice it to say the bad guy turning out to be a good guy has become something of a TV trope, dubbed by many as the Heel-Face Turn. The villain needs someone good enough not to just combat his or her evil but to participate in exposing his inner light. Loving our enemies is good advice after all. Hard as it is, it's saved multiple planets in at least two galaxies in just the last few decades.

They say love is blind . . . There is nothing so clear-sighted as love!
—Anthony de Mello

A blind man came to Jesus. This might always be the accurate way to describe first encounters with the Divine. Jesus forwent snapping his fingers to fix the man's eyes and instead employed a little bit of theater. He spit on the ground and made a dollop of mud. Then he smeared this mud on the man's eyelids. Then he asked the man to review the bizarre operation.

"Umm . . . ," said the man, squinting, confused. "I can see. Uhh, but, so far as I can tell, I am seeing people as walking trees."

The disciples must have looked at each other, concerned. Did Jesus just botch a miracle?

Jesus touched the man again. "How about now?"

"Wow! Now I see things as they are!"

Because there is a kind of seeing that lacks, shall we say, that *second touch*. That deeper layer that transcends the eye's limitations and helps us really observe reality. Perceiving, not just looking. That touch of Christ, that brush with Love himself that helps us to honestly evaluate our first impression of others, to remain aware of our projected, limited understanding that wants to lodge itself in our minds as the truth. Love, on request, touches our eyes again and helps us see a far clearer, far more comprehensive picture. To see things as they are, not as we first interpreted them. The difference between these two could save humanity.

And perhaps this is a place to grow in prayer, not asking

God for circumstances to change as much as for eyes to really see the people who populate those circumstances. Imagine the one who can take up the case for a mean dog, explaining to you that the snarling thing was abused. Imagine seeing the terrible animal transform before your eyes from something that's evil and needs to be put down to something that Love can tame, even make a loyal companion out of. Imagine now it's not a dog but the Image of God.

To ask for Compassion enough to at least imagine another's prequel, their backstory behind this woefully incomplete moment I'm tempted to judge. To request the power to resist rendering judgment quickly, although it makes me feel better to make up my mind about you, what you are, what you want, and all that. To Love enough to really see—to beg God for eyes that do *more than see*, but compassionately observe, as only healthily adjusted self-interest can allow.

Our undisciplined, uncalibrated selfish brains avoid a knowledge gap so vehemently that this ambiguity registers in our neurology as fear. Not knowing things is genuinely uncomfortable. So we fill in the gaps. But we don't do so positively because that's naive and leaves us at risk. We fill the gaps instantly with something negative or prejudiced or unfair and that's that. Putting *something* in the context hole is better than nothing, and making that something a thing to protect yourself from is even better. Ah, figuring someone out is such sweet, misinformed relief.

But this is not really seeing. This is generally making up crap about people with half-truths or less so our undisciplined brains can feel better. It's mud-caked eyes primed for a second touch from the one who grants awakened observation. But we have to ask. We have to repent enough to know those aren't actually tree people out there, so we should stop blaming them for being so. We'll only ask for renewed eyes when we understand that this is exactly what we're hoping everyone else will do for us. Understand that I didn't mean to be hurtful or rude. I had a headache. My back hurts. Know that I was doing the best I could, even though the results were terrible. Had I known then what I know now. Give me a second chance. I had a crappy childhood. I just lost a parent. I'm being audited. I have a terrible temper I don't know how to address yet. Please judge me more by my intentions rather than solely by my actions. *Love me enough to suspend judgment and assume you've got me all wrong, and that there is more to get to know. Together, we'll assume neither of us are trees and keep asking for the ability to see what is.*

We don't see things as they are, we see them as we are.
—Anaïs Nin

21

→

There was evening
and there was morning . . .

WE WERE OVERLOOKING THE CARIBBEAN from our cliff-side table, our day of mission work planned. It was only morning, but the tropical heat was already thickening the ocean air like flour does gravy.

Our bellies full of a Haitian spaghetti breakfast and our hearts full of tropical beauty, we stood up and shouldered our backpacks.

"Oh my God."

One in our group had just been emailed and was staring in shock at his phone. We froze, a few of us daring to ask. He skimmed the email and then summarized it for us aloud. A famous international recording artist's daughter had just been killed.

"His five-year-old daughter was accidentally run over and killed yesterday in her own driveway," he said, grimacing. "Their own SUV, driven by her brother."

We gasped. Along with tens of thousands of others who immediately recognized the countless layers of agony, we gasped.

We shook our heads at each other for a few minutes. One was visibly tearful. A few prayed awkward, fragmented prayers. Finally, we decided to get on with our day and began filing back through the open-air lobby toward the parking lot to load our supplies and depart for our work site. I was in the rear of the line, and I was stopped.

"Is it not magnificent?"

The woman's accent wasn't Haitian. It was French. She was the owner of the hotel at which our team was staying. She had an air of sophistication and confidence, her arms folded, her right hand gripping mango juice, a lit cigarette in her left. She was staring just past me, transfixed.

"Isn't what magnificent?" I said as the rest of the group walked on.

"The plant," she answered, nodding behind me. A tall tropical plant grew from the middle of the terrace around which the tables were arranged. Its large, green fronds each broad enough to conceal a child. "In all the years I have been here, I can never stop appreciating how perfect this plant is."

Her accent made the plant seem like an exhibition. I looked again at the plant I had just walked by. She was right; it *was* perfect. Consummate symmetry, one side a flawless mirror of the other. The leaves so green and healthy it appeared plastic. It could have been the three-dimensional logo for the species. Perfection.

"Wow," I said, mindful I was separated from the team physically and emotionally now. "It's really . . . really amazing."

"And, more than this, we were *made* to appreciate such beauty. It is all really magnificent, no?"

I nodded absently, torn between two worlds.

She held up her mango juice. "Well, *au revoir.*"

Jesus's cousin John the Baptizer had been thrown in jail for telling the truth to the powers that distorted it. Power structures often count on not being seen naked. John had barely been processed and fingerprinted before Jesus was picking up where he'd left off.

He began proclaiming "the gospel," the Good News. This, as his original hearers would've recognized, was the very language of war, or more specifically, war's end. Heralds came back from the war front in those pre–Breaking News Alert days to announce a conflict had ended favorably. Fighting had ceased. Loved ones would be reunited. This information brought back home from the front was called *the gospel.*

Jesus announced Good News just as his beloved cousin was incarcerated for the crime of candor. You and I might have called Jesus's timing insensitive.

But this is our world. This is our faith.

Good things always available in the midst of the bad. Beauty stained by horror. Liberty pocked with injustice. Verdant fields concealing bones of the fallen beneath. Astonishing, symmetrical trees and the unwitting souls they fall upon. If Christ really came to show us how to live, then of course he must teach us to find good news while bad news is happening in his own family. To see the good while acknowledging the acrid smell of the bad, and to neither feel guilty or naive about holding both.

It is an act of Compassion to grieve with those who grieve. To listen and understand what it is that makes people feel like there's nothing left to get out of bed for. To do otherwise is often the delusional self-protective act of denial.

Yet.

Love also embraces the creative power the universe runs on and suggests, "As we acknowledge the difficulty of life, let's never forget we're still describing something we're calling Life!" Love shows up while you're in bed and says, "Coffee? Walk? Hope?" until you finally take her up on it.

We cry real tears and hug each other blue. But we also recognize our joy is an act of resistance in a Kingdom that overthrows with goodness, rather than more to cry about.

Joy is the uprising.

Paul said Love bears and believes and hopes all things. Which is as close as one can get to saying, "Love makes us each a naive Pollyanna" without it starting to seem like the case. Love's toes are on a line here. It's seemingly aware it may look silly to the self-assured cynic and yet is so seeing of reality that "denial" can't legitimately be leveled at it. Love is too strong to simply offer wishful thinking like morphine to the terminal.

> *Love . . . bears all things, believes all things,*
> *hopes all things, endures all things. Love never fails.*
> —Paul, and most wedding officiants,
> 1 Corinthians 13:4–8 NASB

Love chooses to keep itself unflinchingly attuned to real pain while risking the belief that things are still, in the last analysis, good. That precious little girl died at the hands of her own family's mistake. Their hearts will never be the same. And yet those hearts and those hands are no less a part of the beautiful symphony that swells over eons to triumphant climax. "To Life," the Jewish people have toasted one another for millennia, even in the face of unspeakable hardship. They've always known Love never fails.

We despair when we lose people and jobs and relationships. When plans fall through. When the bottom falls out. The word *despair* literally comes from the idea of hope *falling down*. Like a building I can no longer live in. I give up and say, "My best days are behind me. It's over." For a season, maybe this is the only option that has any merit. Telling me not to might just piss me off and make things worse. Especially if you tell me my despair is evidence of my lack of faith.

Then there is hope. *Hope* has the artless etymology of *hop*, which implies it has us choose to keep moving, and risk looking silly doing it. Though our pain is real, it moves forward under even the weakest conviction that the universe is ultimately benevolent if its Author is Love. If I believe and live in the flow of Love, I allow for both despairing and hoping, yet with a preference for bending toward the gravity of the latter. Martin Luther King Jr. seemed to be saying the same when he famously said, "The arc of the moral universe is long, but it bends toward justice." Those sensitive folks who can name Hell and still see Heaven on the horizon, that's what we're invited to be. It's hard to type that sentence, but Jesus and the owner of a Haitian hotel (the hotel, by the way, was later destroyed in an earthquake) tell me that this hop(p)ing is the better story to tell.

Loving others is finding a way to honor the dignity of their experience of pain while simultaneously, respectfully giving them the gift of our own expanded context, the longer view if we have it to offer. When life hits the fan, Love and Hope serve as humble acts of creativity. Acts of gentle building from ruins. "Beauty from ashes," as the saying goes. Jesus was, after all, rumored to be a carpenter—one who takes dead trees and busted stone and builds homes and patios and dinette sets. We continue this inspired trade by respecting what's fallen down as well as respecting that we are creators made in the image of a Creator. Hope is on our side. I know that doesn't make it easy. And hearing this at the wrong time is little more than the salt of the earth meddling in your wounds. It's exhausting carrying the weight of beauty and hardship at the same time. But it's a lie to only carry one. So we, as Paul instructed, carry one another's loads, together. All the light and all the shadow, for richer and for poorer, in sickness and in health, together.

But, just like hopping and building do, hope takes work. Cynicism and despair are far easier, and are often to be preferred. They say a smile takes less muscle than a frown, but frankly, I've found a blank stare is the least effort of all. However, this work of hope, the carpentry of Love when things fall down, is what makes tangible my belief that the news from the front is, in the balance, more Good than anything. So I employ an amphibiousness that holds in tension wrongfully imprisoned John the Baptist and assurances from the Author of Life that great stories require sucky chapters. Love bears both, for its own sake and for others'. There is death and there is life. Random chaos and magnificent symmetry. Crying and laughing, all contextualized on a spinning planet of plants and deserts, peaks and valleys, ever rotating toward and away from the light of the sun.

Strap on your pack.

Au revoir.

22

A Love that's intents

SUSPEND YOUR DISLIKE for the most sleazy lawyers for a moment. And if you are a lawyer of any description, suspend your awareness of what you do the best you can as you read.

Imagine someone you know got arrested for kicking in several storefront windows. It was his first offense of any kind, no one was injured, but criminal damaging being a second-degree misdemeanor, he's facing thousands in fines and six months in jail.

Imagine you are somehow offered a chance to free him. All you have to do is explain what happened in terms that will persuade a judge that it's not as bad as it seems. And if you can explain it satisfactorily, not only will your acquaintance be released, but you also will be rewarded a million dollars.

Don't worry for a second about the moral implications.

Could you do it? As in, do you possess the creativity to make the case?

Might you possess the creative vigor to contextualize the act in such a way so as to get the man out of trouble and you into seven digits worth of cash? Could you tell the story in a way that turned the tide of judgment? Could you spin it as a momentary lapse of reason that need only result in his replacing the windows, not in his having a criminal record and yet another occupied jail cell? Could you argue that he was, for all we know, killing venomous spiders with his boot a little too zealously, though ultimately for our good? "The spiders are bad this year after all, Your Honor." Could you offer to pay for the windows and associated lost revenue in exchange for dismissal of charges—*you'd soon have the cash for it*—promising to take him to anger management classes? "We all need help with our anger, Your Honor . . . Isn't this arrangement far better for his long-term correction than incarceration and a rap sheet anyway?"

Couldn't you find a way to fight for him by applying the best, most positive intent and outcome?

Now imagine they were *your* windows he kicked in.

Wouldn't you, despite this new twist, still possess all the same creative vigor? You'd certainly have the same incentives. And wouldn't you likely have even more leverage, since you're the victim who is, surprising as it is for those watching and expecting judgment-as-usual, seemingly not victimized? And couldn't you, if we stop talking about windows kicked in and some hypothetical courtroom and start talking about the actual people in your home, school, and office, apply the same creative vigor to find a way to make right what needs to be made right without the desire to inflict retribution? We don't really believe victim energy is necessarily stronger than the spirit of forgiveness, do we?

Ask it this way: If it wasn't a million-dollar incentive but was instead the true reconciling and freeing power of Love, would you be any less able to fight for the forgiveness of others—even those who have made trouble very specifically for *you*?

If the answer is suddenly no when it was yes before, then maybe you're more ready to for*sell* than to for*give*. And so now you know an area in which you might want to petition Love to help you.

When you hurt someone, unless you're a sociopath—in which case I'll assume you lost interest many chapters back—you hope that when it comes to judgment your *intentions* will trump your *actions*. We naturally add to our apologies, "I didn't mean to," or "I really didn't think about how that would affect you." Even if there are real, tangible consequences for what you did, and there often should be, you're confident that if the other knew your intentions, it would reduce their bad feelings and increase the probability of reconciliation.

It's a plea for the internal, unseen context behind a (mis)behavior to be considered by the other before sentencing. It matters deeply to us what we intended, and we hope the wounded other will appreciate it. It makes all the difference. It hurts and offends when some woman stomps on your toe on the bus. "Watch out, lady!" But then you look up and see that she is very old and blind. The same physical pain is being experienced, but the place the encounter is processed in your head moves and you can instantly absolve her of guilt. There *isn't* any guilt. Even as your toe throbs the same as it did ten seconds ago, the lack of intent can *cancel* the debt.

And yet, as much as we hope our intentions will be considered most eagerly, and as much as the blind lady would get a pass because it's so easy to tell she didn't mean it, we tend to judge others 180 degrees from what we hope or demand from others. "Forget context and intentions," we're saying now. "What you did and what it did to me are all I care to consider. Excuses, excuses."

I've found I don't really always want justice. I want revenge. But I call my revenge justice. I am a creator made in the image of the Creator, but instead of creating opportunities for reconciliation or explanations that include intent, I sustain the often uncreative pathway for vengeance. I make for me, but destroy you.

The Spirit of Compassion is blowing in our society's air, though that sweet Wind has been hard to notice in this current moment. The winds of tension and division have made us run for cover. But when this moment passes, and it will, we'll pick up where we left off: working to see one another, to celebrate what unites, and to continue growing out of what divides. We're too taken by the idea that if what the previous generation threw away can now be recycled, maybe people are that redeemable too. That someone's story is worth listening deeply to, despite everyone else just wanting their minds made up so they can move on. That perhaps it's slower and more a draw on our emotions, but that perhaps all human beings—ourselves in the mix—are more than the sum of our conclusions. Will we dare to create space for reconciliation and redemption to happen? Will I fight to assume the best in you and stay with you, even when doing so costs me something?

This is no small endeavor for us here in the US. We post the Ten Commandments on courthouse buildings but never the Sermon on the Mount. It seems childish to try to let the Way of

Jesus—the one we refer to as the Lord of all reality—upend our society with Love. How can we achieve anything following an enemy-forgiving, Grace-doling Lord?

Many of us have suffered at the hands of others. Scratch that: every one of us has; it's just a matter of scale. For all of us, there really are things to forgive others for. Maybe not so much things as people who made the things happen. I've found I can't really forgive an event, I have to forgive the person who did it. If you burn down my house, I can't forgive the fire, despite it being the thing that was so bad. So I forgive you, who must have had reasons, whether or not I agree with them, for doing such a thing. It will take work, some Compassion, some seeing, some creativity, and it will take several (hundred?) attempts. But I will be forgiving toward you. I will let you off of every hook I recognize my mind hanging you on. The alternative is you burning down my house as well as burning down my happiness and my hope and my will to be free of your actions. And that's far too much to give to anyone.

You and I have the power to pardon, to release, more than we give ourselves credit for. More than perhaps we can be credited for. We are, after all, made in the image of a boundless giver of Love, and not in the image of a wounded, unsettled account. Do we believe this or not? I have enough faith that I can be forgiven, so it might stand to reason—if I'm following that Golden Rule—that I can forgive you too.

Our Father in heaven
Wholly Other be Your Reputation
Your Kingdom, Your Way, be in effect in our living

Give us today our plenty
And forgive us our infliction of pain
As we simultaneously forgive the pain inflicted upon us
Lead us around the temptation to make this chiefly about
    ourselves
Rescue us from becoming the evil that's happened to us
Amen.

NOTES

PART SIX

Undebted

Forgiveness is the final form of love.

Reinhold Niebuhr

23

Paralysis

IT WAS STANDING ROOM ONLY. Jesus and the boys were back in town. Hearing this, everyone showed up at the house to take in his wisdom and bask some in both his presence and in his rising profile.

Five friends got there late. Who could blame them, considering four of them had to carry the paralyzed fifth. Their friend couldn't walk, and out of something ranging from compassion for their unfortunate friend to the reasonably selfish desire to start getting all five of them to parties on time, the friends carried him to Jesus to see if the teacher could heal him.

When they found the door blocked and even the windows obscured by eager listeners, they improvised. Climbing the outside stairs of the home, they carried their friend up to the roof and yanked some of the tiles out. Jesus's sermon was suddenly interrupted by the limp form of a man in a halo of sunlit dust dropping through the ceiling.

A few close to Jesus sprang to assist the human marionette safely to the floor. The friends looked down through the unrequested hatch, nervous about Jesus's potential irritability. Jesus smiled back at them. Acts of courageous, innovative Compassion always trump a sermon. One read through the Gospels shows a Jesus who sermonized far less than those who lead his church. There in the middle of the room lay a crippled, motionless man in the glow of a makeshift skylight. What did the Healer say to a man needing healed?

Heavenly Father, heal his legs.

Alakazam.

Neither.

He said, "Son, your sins are forgiven." Jesus went first into the man's mind while everyone else stared at his withered feet. I hate it when God doesn't address the problems I present. I suppose it's possible that Jesus was forgiving the very recent sin of vandalism to his home. But would a miracle-working carpenter be too worried about a hole in the roof? This was about something else.

An immediate sense of scandal arose for the biblically educated men in the room. Forgiving sins is God's jurisdiction. This Jesus was a good teacher, but he was playing with fire now. Jesus asked them about it, knowing their thoughts. And after a religious debate failed to get off the ground, the paralyzed man did. Jesus had the man "arise."

The same word used elsewhere in the New Testament for those waking up and getting out of bed. The same word used to describe the dead living again. *Resurrection.*

The paralytic man was a man who couldn't walk. But the story isn't chiefly a story of a man having his legs healed as though that's the programmed outcome of forgiveness. I'm sure there have been plenty paralytic readers of this story who have accepted that there are depths to plumb beyond the plain reading. And those depths might go like this: the paralyzed man's guilt and shame, and the burden of condemnation that renders us all unable to "walk," needed to be lifted.

"Son," said Jesus tenderly to a man whom the text depicts as being toted around by friends rather than family, "your sins have been cast out. You're free."

Then, and only then apparently, can the man arise and take responsibility for his journey. His burden of guilt was damaging himself, not Christ. This is always the case. Always.

To the man lying motionless on Christ's rug, and to us, he says,

You know you're forgiven, right?
You know you don't have to be a slave to the lowest impulses of
*   yourself and society anymore?*
You know the shame you carry wasn't assigned to you by anyone
*   with authority?*
Off the floor, son!
Get up, daughter!
Stand up and walk!
Resurrect now, don't wait!
You're free! Go and freely be this same healing Love!

I can't count how many times I have marinated in simmering remorse for days—months!—because I was sure I had hurt someone with my words. With a forgotten date. With an offhand comment made about someone who wasn't in the room but who heard about it later. Then I am face-to-face with them, the consequences of my lack of consideration burning in my chest, paralyzing me. Even making me feel anger that seems to have no reasonable place to go but into the chest of the very person I had already hurt.

And they say, "Dude, it's no big deal at all. I never gave it a second thought."

Or, "Yeah, it stung a little, but I got over it. Seriously, we're cool."

Or, "Yes, I'm still upset. I still don't know why you did that. But thank you for apologizing. Maybe we can talk more about it later. I'm grateful you said something."

Suddenly I'm on my feet rather than stuck on my back. Formerly lifeless limbs of the body tingling, renewing their connection as unique but integrated parts of the whole. Movement returns. I'm not necessarily all better, but I'm at least off my mat and ready to help fix holes in roofs and anything else that's happened because of me.

And I give this same gift to others when I forgive. When I forgive, I relieve a burden and put you and me back on our feet, together. We are, as people of faith, a liberation people after all, given the power to liberate. Love made in the image of Love to do what Love does: free captives. Forgiveness is an Exodus, while withheld forgiveness is a hard-hearted keeping of slaves.

If you forgive others for their wrongdoings, your heavenly Father will also forgive you. But if you do not forgive, don't pretend you get to participate halfway in the circuitry of Grace.
—From Jesus's words, after the Lord's Prayer,
Matthew 6:14–15, my rendering

24

Billy Joel sang it best

MY FRIEND RICH AND I agreed to help our mutual pal Patrick build his barn for a couple of days. It is to date the most Amish week of my life.

There we were, thirty feet in the air, straddling still-naked trusses of two-by-fours as we banged away at the frame. My main concern was not falling to my death. The other two seemed to be more attuned to the work at hand. But Patrick soon proved less focused on driving in nails as he was with something else.

As we joked and told stories, Patrick kept looking over at Rich and shaking his head, agitated. After half an hour he was out with it.

"Richard. Your belt is on crooked. The nail pouch should be on the front."

Rich looked down and made a face. He wasn't concerned. Patrick waited a couple of minutes and tried again.

"If you have it where it goes, you can pull nails out more easily. More safely. See?" he said, demonstrating with his own.

Rich assured him, "Got it. This is fine, though."

Another two or three minutes of hammers banging filled the quiet.

"Richard, dude, spin it around correctly," Patrick said.

Rich gave me a glance. Why was Patrick concerning himself with the placement of the nail pouch on someone else who was fine with where it was?

Bang, bang, bang.
Bang, bang, bang, bang.
Bang, bang, bang, bang, bang.

"RICHARD! Just. Ugh. Here!" Patrick was now sprawling across the beams and twisting the belt around Rich's waist into its proper place, speaking through his teeth as he did. Rich held his hammer, bracing himself on the trusses as he was jostled, staring at Patrick, then staring at me. "There! It goes like that!" Patrick was yelling.

Rich and I didn't return the next day. Later I saw the barn and assumed it was *exactly* how Patrick wanted it.

It's not that anyone had committed a specific crime. It was just one of those moments when human beings occupy the same space with different preferences, and no one knew well how to handle it.

The Gospels are missing most of the content many of us have been led to think is there. All the content that has Jesus speaking to people about how they need to be unrecognizably different from how he found them, based on the absolute of divine preference for every life, got erased or something. Or the idea that God is obsessed with us becoming different than we currently are is something we brought to the text, rather than away from it. Yes,

yes, our transformation is strongly in the message, but not how I think we think.

In ninety-nine out of a hundred exchanges, who does Jesus level criticisms to but religious leaders who make it their careers to tell other people to change into something they'll validate. And isn't the rest of Jesus's time spent healing people who are demonstrably not what they could be—people who become real beneficiaries of meaningful change that makes them more of what they truly are, not something else that avoids divine criticism?

Missing are the stories of people commanded by Jesus to dress differently in order to showcase a certain set of values. He laughed off that sort of piety. There's no section where Jesus talks about responsible adulthood, or how long you can reasonably live at your parents' house, or how much is too much time playing video games. Stories where Jesus tells people that they need to pick a specific church, back a particular candidate, believe in a certain age of the earth. We could go on and on. It's almost as if Jesus was okay with people generally having their own way about things. As if morality and socially conditioned preferences weren't a spoken concern. Jesus wanted people to wake up and live in the flow of God's powerfully living Spirit. Everything else got somewhere between silence, a shrug, or the gift of fascination with someone's different opinion.

And if someone in power tried to apply their preferences as though they came from God—a reasonable understanding of what it means to take the Lord's name in vain—Jesus had some strong words:

You Bible teachers travel land and sea to convert
a single person and in doing so make them
twice an accursed son as you are.
—Matthew 23:15, my rendering

I've been persuaded in recent years that forgiveness isn't just letting people off the punitive hook for a specific thing they have done to me. That is its own effort, to be sure. But forgiveness is more than this; not just more in effort but in significance.

Forgiveness is a signal that radiates outward to people like a public service announcement that, rather than anyone being asked to be stronger in their performance for me, I will be stronger in my acceptance of whatever performance is offered. It's the moment-to-moment charitableness that doesn't hold my unmet preferences against others. I think of it as the higher part of me apologizing for the lower: "Sorry about my silly demander and his demands on you. Just ignore him, because they are not as valid as he thinks they are. Carry on." This form of forgiveness is less about a specific crime against me and my reaction to it, and more a sweeping kindness, a bioluminescent glow in the dark that allows people to be what they are and me to be what I am independent of that, best I can. For those of us who grew up in critical environments that shamed and teased us into acting differently, it's a Loving decision to remain in the flow of suspended expectations. A smile in the face of humanity's perfected defectiveness.

Patrick couldn't stand where the belt hung on Richard. He couldn't let it go—couldn't forgive it—because his preferences felt more like rules. But I suppose Patrick has a specific way he wants things to be. That's just *his way*. Who am I to tell him to be otherwise? Why not just adjust the belt and move on? Surely Patrick's affection for precision makes for better barns than I could build. As much as I can blame him for not forgiving so silly a thing like a belt that needed a quarter turn, why can't I forgive his need for control over such trivialities? There we were, suspended in the air, a few yards closer to Heaven, frustrated with each other for being so different from how we wanted.

I don't mean to imply that the goal is to pretend not to care about anything. I've chased my tail there. The goal, I think, is to recognize how badly we want control that we don't have, and how profoundly we want people to change themselves because then they'd be less work. When we tell someone we love them, that should mean forever, a promise from the heart . . .

I could not love you any better
I love you just the way you are
–Billy Joel, "Just the Way You Are"

This inability to forgive others for being other than we'd prefer is one more way we treat others opposite from what we want in return. This starts early. You can see it on a middle school playground when the new kid's shoes aren't to standard, costing her inclusion and love. The other kids will actually say "ew" to feign disgust. They believe they are being offended by their preferences not being adhered to. The "ew" is a group expulsion, the kid getting puked out of the club like bad milk from a body. There's no specific crime or victim. The kid has simply failed an inspection with manufactured consequence. But what's required is a kind of charitableness, a forgiveness that learns to acknowledge the preferences announcing themselves in our minds but refuses to hold those unmet preferences against the other. Children do well to learn one really has nothing to do with the other!

But it doesn't stop with children. You can see it in adults when they hear the words *Republican* or *Democrat*, depending on their election predilections. They can become angry at the mere name of the incumbent, or angry at anger toward the incumbent. In their mind they are being wronged at the very mention of an alternative worldview. Red-faced and clipped in the wings. Yet there's no real crime. There is, however, the same opportunity to offer a charitableness that doesn't hold unmet preferences against the other for their views. If we cannot radiate forgiveness of difference, and even dignify that difference, then we may never make it off the playground. We'll have fallen prey to that silly illusion that children unthinkingly assume is true: different perspectives mean we're different beings, and only one being can be king of the mountain.

Compassion, among so many other things we can understand it to be, is that sacred *together suffering*, that expanded maturity that is able to absorb other people's consistent track record for not being just how I want them to be. Let's be honest: I'm not even exactly how I want me to be.

"I don't need you to be any different than who you are" might be a good mantra to whisper to our own minds as we encounter our spouse or kids or manager or others on the subway. "I forgive you for not being me, or the *you* I might childishly prefer. And if I *do* need you to be different, well, now we're talking about my weakness, not yours."

Perhaps a sign that we have been empowered from on high to do something inspired is that we can Love one another, just the way we are. A power not so much like an alchemy of turning water to wine but of an expanded appreciation for water just as it is. So take a second and pray thus: *God, help me perform the miracle of drinking what's poured, not only what I've transformed into something I prefer the taste of. For surely, as it pertains to human beings, this is the true miracle of Compassion.*

25

Forgiving you for
being you allows you
to be the real you

NONE OF US enjoys a two-faced person. A manipulator. A conniver. A dissembler.

But who else is there to Love?

If we're going to Love people, then we're going to have to be honest and say this is how most people are. Our lack of forgiveness—practiced in our demands that others be and do *something else* before we'll be at peace with them—creates the cautious duplicity we hate in the first place.

> *To be fully seen by somebody, then, and be loved anyhow—*
> *this is a human offering that can border on miraculous.*
> —Elizabeth Gilbert

The television series *V* was a huge hit my third-grade year. But I wasn't.

I didn't understand the social requirements for becoming popular. So I did what any socially inept, eight-year-old sci-fi enthusiast would do to try to garner friends and belong. I drew scales on my arm with a Sharpie and covered it with peach construction paper and tape. When kids came by who I hoped would eventually deem me worthy of a birthday party invitation or a kind word, I'd rip the paper off and hiss at them. Astoundingly, no kindness was awarded these special effects. Earthlings.

In fourth grade I experienced my problem more acutely. I was rich in imagination but destitute on social know-how. Blessed are the poor? *Hmph*. Drawing aliens with my colored-pencil set was easy. Drawing a crowd that didn't want to harm me for the sport of it, harder. I needed to adjust their attention toward me to something positive, to compensate for my odd looks (their words) and odder interests (same here). Einstein observed that problems aren't solved by the level of consciousness that create them. Which is probably why my solution made so much sense to me and garnered so few positive results.

I began telling kids my real name wasn't Steve. It was Rex. *Rex*, of course, is Latin for "king" and was also my favorite dinosaur's surname. I was Rex Daugherty. This had all the relational

Mighty T-Rex, 4th grade

magnetism of construction paper skin and a flitting tongue. It turns out dinosaur kings have *less* appeal to the upper echelons of fourth-grade hierarchy, not more. Back to the drawing board.

In fifth grade I had a burgeoning reputation as an artist. *The weird kid with the oversized cranium can draw.* Something like that. I vividly remember the day I sketched a scene from *Star Wars* and, before I could rationally process the decision, found myself sliding it across the table to Michael. Michael was a popular kid who spoke to me here and there. But he would also, without warning or provocation, lead attacks against me. This left me in ambiguous anxiety over whether he was an enemy or not. For a desperate fifth grader, this ambiguity might have been more psychologically dangerous than consistent hostility.

Michael took the drawing, a carefully sketched take on Jabba's Palace, replete with his minions, and carefully placed it in his folder like a precious ancient manuscript. I was stunned. Stunned I'd shared it, and stunned he'd received it with such care.

At the end of the day our class would line up for the final bell. Scholarly types by the door, cool kids in the middle, leprous losers in the back huddled by the coatrack. As I made my way to the tail of this social creature, Michael stopped me.

"You wanna cut?" he said.

Assuming he was either talking to his round-tipped scissors or was joking at my expense, I didn't respond. When he repeated himself, it was suddenly clear I was experiencing what I believe might have been the first invitation of my life. Then Aaron, a head taller than Michael, whose hostility was graciously consistent, spoke up with disgust on his breath. Aaron had a mustache and was rumored to have already fathered a child.

"You're letting *him* cut?" Aaron said to Michael.

I looked at Michael to see what he would say. It never occurred to me that I had every right to cut in line if so invited. I waited to hear Michael defend himself, not me. Hey, I was just as surprised as Aaron.

"Yeah, I am," Michael said. He reached into his folder and pulled out my drawing. "He drew me this."

Aaron rolled his eyes and backed off. At least the spot in line had been purchased. Otherwise he'd have to object. His clique couldn't bear suddenly becoming charitable toward kids with the lingering reputation of being lizards with paper skin.

I shuffled into the middle of the line where jeans fit correctly, kids chose their own haircuts, and Stacy's up-close beauty could be confirmed in the absence of the caste buffer. As I stepped out of the margins and into the median, waves of revelation swept over me: I had converted their opinions. By George (Lucas) I'd finally figured it out. How to compensate for all the insufferable, unpardonable facets of what made Rex, Rex. I finally knew how to make up for all I'd learned was unforgivable about me.

You probably learned this too. I have the impulse to offer what can only be considered an entertaining product, buying my way into your acceptance since, as was solidified decades ago, I may not have what it takes apart from this offering. Maybe you use charm, intellect, cleavage, biceps, cash, humor, soup kitchens, condescension, compliments, undaunted effervescence, witty cynicism. I'm using the word *use* here. These facets of our exterior aren't inherently bad. They're just not as intrinsic, being instead an act we were driven to by the unforgiveness of others also trying to find a way to get by. A big show none of us wants to be in and yet none of us can clearly determine how to get out of.

Being "saved" has so much more to do with right now than the postmortem arrangement the American Christian tradition has long focused on. And we humans of every religious description need to be saved. Saved, rescued, delivered, as in accepting the Acceptance shown to us in an unoffended Christ. Being gracious enough to allow others to be whatever they are, or not be what they aren't, so that—for God's sake—nobody starts trying to purchase and act their way into the middle of our lines. Mercy over sacrifice. This is a legitimate way of describing what has been done for us who follow this Christ: transformed by the invitation, rather than transformed to get an invitation. Nothing has transformed me like those beautiful people who never demanded I transform. I try to pass this gift to others.

We can be rescued, made free—just as the Christ said the naked truth would set us—and find ourselves newly able to let others be annoying. Be wrong. Be unattractive. Misguided. Angry. Unfunny. Untraditional. Not of our tribe. Naive. And in all of this we remain what we are: vessels of Love and Truth who do not incentivize others to earn what is free. This is the work of Compassionate Forgiveness. The Spirit of Grace liberating others through us, delivering them from the sense of safety their performance used to give them. Now they can come closer to being just one person. One and known, rather than multiple and alone.

But we can't step into any of this as long as we believe our preferences—our take on morality, our truths, the way we like to be treated, our kingdom reigning at home and at work and in the nation—must be satisfied. Not only will we *not* get what we demand, which is its own misery, we will continue to motivate people to be the pretending, performing actors we find it so hard to love anyway—a second misery. Who doesn't want hypocrisy and pretense to come to an end? But who among us is willing to do the work of acceptance required to put those things away for good?

Consider that maybe forgiveness takes the world largely as it is and then enjoys the change that unfolds as a result of accepting it. This doesn't mean I don't talk about my faith or my reasons  for thinking and believing as I do or get involved if someone needs help or is hurting themselves. Neither is this an ode to apathy, where we look at all the work needing to be done in this world, done for the people who live in it with great difficulty, and announce indifference in Christ's name. On the contrary, this is all our growing conviction that taking each other as we are is how we are finally able to stop living defensively against those attempting to control us. Instead, how about we walk together and see what marks we leave on one another as the trust required of us by Love exposes far more than our apparent differences? Perhaps we can find in an involved, earnest acceptance what has been hidden by forcing others to pay for their spot in line.

A friend is someone who gives you total freedom to be yourself—
and especially to feel, or not feel. Whatever you happen
to be feeling at any moment is fine with them.
That's what real love amounts to—
letting a person be what he really is.
—Jim Morrison

26

Forgiving my idols

JESUS STOOD ON THE MOUNTAINSIDE and was about halfway through his sermon. He'd said much to this point. More than anyone could digest in one sitting. Now he was telling his diverse audience, the rich and the poor, the upper and lower class alike, not to worry.

"Don't worry about your life," he said. "What you'll eat or drink or wear."

The rich were hearing Jesus say something about major elements of their social lives.

The poor were hearing something about the sort of things that made them feel desperate.

Everyone was hearing something about what populates too much of their thinking, and too much of their ranking of others as well.

He didn't suggest we have no concern at all for having basic necessities. Surely the majority of Maslow's hierarchy of needs gets a Divine nod. But he went on to say birds have food and that flowers are beautiful without the distinctly human trait of having anxiety over maintaining this food and beauty.

Jesus told his students not to live anxiously like the Gentiles do in making his point. Gentiles, those outsiders and pagans who were understood to be not as well acquainted with the Love and peace of God, are the ones who lived with this angst about how they were doing. They didn't have the compass that Jesus's audience did. At least not one outside of their grumbly gut and their twitchy amygdalae. "Everyone here on this mountainside constitutes a people of faith in God," Jesus was saying. "You seek to do life differently, meaningfully, rightly. Well, sometimes I can't tell the difference between you and those you tend to judge as outsiders when I watch how you claw through a day."

As long as I worry that I am not okay, that I may actually be owed better than I'm getting, that my happiness is around the corner but can't be found on this block, I begin to be someone looking for a thing I already have. One looking there, or there, for the thing that's right here—a mindless idiot searching for the glasses sitting on top of his head while angrily blaming others for stealing them. When I become this way, owed and unfulfilled, I subtly—and then overtly—expect you all to come through for me.

But you won't. You never really do when it comes to my making you responsible for my human happiness. No one can reasonably blame you.

Neither will I come through for you in any soul-fulfilling way. Let's be honest.

And so now, here we all are, desperate for survival, slighted by all the disappointing failures everyone else has proven to be. You failed me. You can't be trusted. You can't be used the way I need you to let me use you. You said you were going to be there for me, but then there was that one time you weren't, and so I feel I must make you pay for that the rest of our lives. Everything is a damnable transaction when I think people are competing for the same limited resources on a deserted island. And if you don't pay, what good are you?

And soon, something good about the human experience fully contorts into a utilitarian nightmare.

Your appearance now *has* to be attractive, because I need to be seen with the very best of the species. If you can be considered less attractive, you can be considered less useful to that level of consciousness. If you're downright ugly, you're a liability.

Of course I need you to find me attractive for these same reasons. But also found pleasing in personality in the bargain, lest I rank as *shallow*. So I will "act like a gentleman," as they say.

Additionally, your attitude must be not too negative, while not overly cheery, as I need people who make interactions with me to tax me as little as possible. Just be cool.

I often don't know how I am going to get through a day, so I need people around who I am sure can help me, while disposing of those who will create problems or drains on my limited resources.

You can be my friend if you make me laugh while also laughing at me to make me feel funny. Also, I'll feel closer to you if you validate me and my interests. Otherwise you can only be an acquaintance or less.

On and on it goes. Reasonable hopes for sane interaction become a pageant, a checklist of anxiety-driven, self-prioritizing values, much of which we're not consciously aware of yet they govern every exchange we have. It feels wholly legitimate that

I am not okay and therefore must recruit people into my strategy for becoming so. They say drowning people are dangerous because, in their desperation, other swimmers become a means to climb out of the water, rather than fellow swimmers.

The verse numbers and chapter breaks in Matthew's gospel were added to the Bible generations after they were first penned. So what is printed as Matthew chapter 6 and Matthew chapter 7 were originally one uninterrupted thought. And at the end of chapter 6 we read Jesus saying that anxiety is bad for us and is unnecessary for the soul awakened to the Love of God. That what we become desperate to seek out in others—and are therefore subsequently disappointed by—is already available to us. "Seek first God's immediately available Kingdom," Jesus said here, "and you will find that what you actually need will be made available outside your desperate worrying about it."

And then chapter 7 continues:

> Do not judge so that you will not be judged. For in the way you judge, you will be judged; and by your standard of measure, it will be measured to you. Why do you look at the speck that is in your brother's eye, but do not notice the log that is in your own eye? Or how can you say to your brother, "Let me take the speck out of your eye," and behold, the log is in your own eye? You hypocrite, first take the log out of your own eye, and then you will see clearly to take the speck out of your brother's eye.

Inviting people not to allow worry to govern their lives, flowing right into the invitation to stop judging others for their shortcomings. It's not that having worry is the crime. Jesus himself sweat blood before the crucifixion, which, I'm told, is about as anxious as a human being can express itself as being. But, as the blood dripped, he prayed, "Not my will but yours be done." Ultimately, as the anxiety swells and rolls inside us, we're invited to be mastered by it no longer. And we're invited to no longer attempt to master others with it as well. To the mind ruled by angst, the world is always less than it has to be for us to feel happy, and so we make a personality out of being robbed of joy. But to the mind ruled by the King of the Kingdom—which isn't supposed to be as detached and floaty as it's come to sound— the world is the very place a happy life can be lived.

Yes, there are many things that cause suffering, real suffering. Things that mustn't fall out of view or go unaddressed because we've confused apathy for *shalom*. And yes, our emotions and the chemical cocktails in our heads have a great deal to say about our experience with joy. We should remember that the one who told us not to worry was of an oppressed minority suffering under the heel of a murderous empire. Somehow, with inspiration, we can learn how to be active, compassionate participants in the real world and enjoy life no matter the outcome. If we won't learn, then there's little else to do with our anxiety than to make others responsible for it. And I don't think that's ever worked for any of us.

"Do not worry" and "do not condemn others" is the same phrase in two frequencies. Listen for it, and you'll see.

The thing I am holding against you probably, definitely, resides in me. Anxious people are deft blamers. Pointing to all the world and finding it at fault, finding it unforgivable. Note here that *blame* is another word for "damn," and it used to be used that way. However, the vast majority of the time, once I can see things as they really are, the speck in your eye reveals itself to be a leaf off the tree in mine. That is, most likely I'm projecting when I blame. What I don't know for certain about you I angrily fill in with things I know about me. So I'm really always failing to see that it's the tree in my own eye I'm pissed at.

> *Everything that irritates us about others*
> *can lead us to an understanding of ourselves.*
> —Carl Jung

The more I learn that others aren't in possession of what I need to be happy, that the Empire of God is others-centered and nontransactional and lies either dormant or awakened in me but not outside of me, the more I begin to forgive you for not "coming through" for me. Coming through for me wasn't your job. If someone has to be blamed, I'll blame this way: I sinned by making you responsible for what God said I'm responsible for. Sorry about that. I'm awake now and won't let it happen again.

It's helpful to think most of my withheld forgiveness and grace toward others can legitimately be catalogued as idolatry. What else is it when I expect you to cure me of my anxiety and work miracles so that I might have my happiness back? Is there anything as unloving, or as crazy, as holding you to a standard I know you can't reach and then blaming you for my sense of disappointment afterward?

Of course, sooner or later, I have to not blame me either. I'm also not God. Sooner or later blame just won't come up anymore, since acceptance is what transforms and frees and gets us unwrapped from the axle, as it were.

But tossing out idols is unnerving. My pharmaceutical relationship with people and the universe has become a habit, one that gets my hands trembling if I don't feed it. To absolve the entirety of the exterior world for it not making me as happy as I thought it could make me always feels like a totally different sort of lived experience. The ancients called it rebirth.

27

→

Diss-ciples

FORGET YOU EVER SAW da Vinci's *The Last Supper*. It's a beautiful work, yes. I'm told you can even replace the pieces of bread dotting the table with musical notes and get a pretty great funeral dirge. But take the painting out of your mind. Because you may have an image in your head where all these men were basically the same. Variations on a theme, different robes and beard thicknesses, but essentially copies of each other. *The apostles.*

Rather than thinking of only Judas as the one dissident—and, of course, that he was—try to see these men for who they were. How they thought.

Peter, Andrew, James, and John. Fishermen who had lately felt forced to fish all day and all night in the overfished Sea of Galilee. With each empty net pulled to the surface, they cursed the Romans more and more for their seeming insatiability for fish and for the empire's little regard for the hands that netted them.

Thomas wasn't so much a doubter as he was a cynic. "Messiahs come and go," was Thomas's skeptical take. Tales of miracles and bold revolutionaries were as common as the bone boxes those bold revolutionaries ended up in. "Might is right, and no one has might like Caesar. Get over it," Thomas might've said to anyone who wondered about God's Kingdom ever being established in the real world.

Simon the Zealot had some inflammatory views about all of this. "You gotta fight fire with fire!" he'd likely say. The Zealots, those nationalists who used religious rhetoric to dress up their desperate thirst for national sovereignty, often carried little daggers in their robes. They'd wait for an opportune time to assassinate prominent names in the market or during a parade, in hopes to foment the unrest needed for the revolution, the overthrow, to begin. Overpower the powers that be. Would God call God's warriors to any less?

Imagine the table, each man sitting there—or lying there, as the custom dictated—complaining, countercomplaining, pointing out the appreciable fact that complaining accomplishes nothing but ulcers. Some spoke of the past. Others dreamt of the future. One on this end of the table quoting his hero, another recoiling at those same words as coming from the devil himself.

Imagine Matthew sitting between them quietly. Matthew's job prior to his joining Team Jesus, of course, was tax collection. The temple had its compulsory offerings and numerous fees for being. This was involuntarily coupled with Roman taxes, which amounted to well over half one's income. Imagine how Jewish men felt about a Jewish man who excised tax on, say, fish. Ancestral land. Grain. All for the empire, hail Caesar, resistance is futile. Imagine how Matthew felt when Simon Z. got out his knife and sharpened it as he talked about what needed to be done about all this. How Matthew felt when the fishermen cursed his employer and the unsustainability of the whole arrangement.

Imagine his leaning into the hushed tones the anglers used when they added a curse to Matthew himself for selling out. Imagine where all this would go without the Uniting One, Love and Compassion and Forgiveness Incarnate, sitting there doling out bread and acceptance and the keys to another kind of Kingdom.

These men had very little reason to ever be found at dinner together. Jesus put weary blue-collars, a swindling government lapdog, and a volatile conspiracy theorist, to name a few, at the same table. Like a three-year, irresponsibly inflammatory arbitration meeting. And before Jesus's crucifixion, he said,

> *A new commandment I give to you, that you love one another:*
> *just as I have loved you, you also are to love one another.*
> *By this all people will know that you are my disciples,*
> *if you have love for one another.*
> —Jesus, John 13:34–35

Why command his guys to Love each other unless their marked differences of opinion were to remain? Don't we sort of automatically Love those who align with our path, whose voice harmonizes with our own? Didn't Jesus imply strongly by making Love a commandment that it was something they would need to be *commanded* to do? You know, in the event that they forgot there is a higher Love than that which can only be offered to people exactly like yourself.

And of all things we people of faith could be known as "disciples" for, and of all the things we *are* known for, is there anything more dignifying of our uniqueness than to be told we have to Love each other, despite our differences?

The command to Love is a subtle promise. A promise that the mantle of our personalities is to be held with grace, because the core of our being is Oneness, even when that Oneness is obscured.

Really, we could have been given the command—and even the supernatural ability—to transform other folks into something aligned with God's template. The gospel at gunpoint, as I attempted in my early twenties for the Lord. Turn or burn. But instead, we're given the command to Love for the very reason that uniformity will never happen.

Observe the table of disciples, and see if you don't recognize that, if left to their own superficial assessment, they have no more business being in that da Vinci painting than you do with whoever it is you clench your jaw about when you hear that person's name. Like those first disciples, those first students, we are students of the one who shows us how Love dignifies difference and unifies us around kindness and light, not around conformity.

And in my experience, when we stay at the table with the self-sacrificial Christ, a certain kind of deep sameness is eventually discovered. That connectedness one often gets, I'm told, when they look at Earth from space. How can a ball with puzzle-piece continents be any less than the home of one family? In the presence of the Unifying One, soon the patriot and the pacifist, the left and the right, the one who looks longingly backward and the one who looks hopefully forward, find their common center. The "y'all" emerges. I don't think any old table can do this. But Christ's, the one bent on a Love we can't catalog as a good idea for only some folks, seems to be a table that can save us all. Whether or not this table is at a church or a bar or a monastery or a dining room or isn't a literal table at all are but details. The Christ has little regard for our geographic constraints.

Every tribe. Every language. Every nation. Jesus looked at people who would argue on a good day and who would attempt murder on a bad day and said, "Stay at this table and I can teach you to Love. Anyone. To honor and respect and dignify them all." I observe as sort of a wonderful joke on us all that he never told those boys which of them was right. All but Love is wrong, I suppose.

But you should know, the command to Love is also a warning: it won't seem to come naturally. At least not at first. We will have to *choose* to suffer the gap between our ideas, our views, and find a deeper oneness than what can be made from mere similarity or agreement. This is the embrace of new instincts, and it takes time. But be merciful and accepting of yourself. The disciples double-dipped in the salsa for years with Jesus and still couldn't get it right. Maybe someday it will become habit. Until then, it's a command. If you listen, you can hear it whispered in your ear right before you say that dumb thing on Facebook or roll your eyes at dinner. "Love, because of difference, not as an alternative to difference."

This command isn't a burden, even as it's challenging. It's

one we welcome. Is there anything more beautiful than wholly disparate people being held in the gravitational pull of Love? Frankly, is there anything remarkable at all about a clique where that gravity isn't required? Let us forgive the supposed sin of dissimilarity. The superficial illusion of separateness. And let us be honest that for now it's easier to forgive somebody for punching you in the eye than for drawing such different conclusions than you have.

NOTES

PART SEVEN

Don't Worry.
Everybody Dies.
Even Death.

Truly, truly, I say to you, unless a grain
of wheat falls into the earth and dies, it remains alone;
but if it dies, it bears much fruit.

Jesus, John 12:24 NASB

28

→

Reality is deciduous

ONE WINTER, ON A TRIP BACK HOME for the holidays, my wife and I were about half an hour into Ohio when she broke the road-weary silence:

"If we were explorers or pioneers, and had no previous understanding that trees do this," she said, pointing to the miles of leafless, dormant trees lining the highway, "can you imagine how it would seem?"

She went on to explain her question.

To the uneducated the whole landscape, stretched in browns under a winter gray sky, would look dead. With the exception of a few pine trees and their sporadic dots of green, everything would appear to have expired. It would seem for those unacquainted with the seasons that something bad had happened. A bomb had gone off. Maybe a great fire had consumed the state. A terrible disease had swept across the whole country, and all but those last green survivors were gone. You would have every reason to believe death had had its way and you'd want out of there.

But we aren't uneducated. Much the opposite; we grew up where there are deciduous and coniferous trees, putting rickety loose lumber houses in and presents beneath them, respectively. So we know almost instinctively that trees do this from about October through March. No sense of fear or grief follows. A vague sense of revulsion if you're as unappreciative of the cold as I am, but not despair.

Just wait, we instinctively think. *Spring is coming. Winter's a season, not a final state.*

Deciduous trees shed their leaves. The Latin *decidere* means to "fall down" or "fall off." Coniferous, or cone-bearing, are evergreens and are ever green. This is kid stuff. We know it like we know about the effects of gravity and beans in our diet. We've always known trees aren't dead when they look so. We assume a cycle without knowing we do, despite *finality* being better supported by the immediate evidence.

Imagine seeing a sunset for the first time as a conscious adult. It wouldn't be beautiful at all. How terrifying that the great source of life-sustaining light and heat was dissolving into the horizon, slowly turning the sky red, then petering out and surrendering to the victory of night. Imagine a child walking up to you in your terror, your hands on your face, tears in your eyes:

"It's okay, sir. It comes back up over there in the morning."

Isn't part of what makes a sunset not terrifying but instead beautiful is that we know about mornings?

People of faith are supposed to be paying very close attention, so that we can be more and more acquainted with the cyclical ways of pain and grief, and of death. Discomfort and hardship can't be avoided—can't even be reduced by prayer, in my general observation—but neither are they final. I've spent so much of my life avoiding falling down or falling off. Because I learned somewhere that falling is The End. I have feared pain and I have feared death. Somewhere, probably like you, I learned life was one great straight line, with an *A* on one end and a *Z* on the other, rather than the circles and cycles and spirals it reveals itself to be.

And as I come to recognize this cyclicality, I am slowly learning to live more deciduously. I think all reality might be so.

In speaking about the temporality of death, Paul rhetorically asked his friends in Corinth, "Where is Death's sting? Where is Death's victory?"

This is an ironic thing for a man who has since completely decomposed to go down in history as having said. But he was only in part speaking about the future state of "Paul." He was also speaking to what happens within us when we come to recognize, with conviction, that death is a nonnegotiable-yet-somehow-revocable reality. And when death becomes penultimate in my mind, then it loses its ability to make me desperate. It becomes a troubling winter, but not final despair. Spring comes next. The sun comes back up over there tomorrow.

I have lived. I will die. But is that A through Z? Only for one new to the area, I'm persuaded.

Jesus gave the picture of a seed falling to the ground to make life. The seed dies, separated from its life source. It is buried, out of view. Obscured. Forgotten. And then it is raised up to new life. This was one way he spoke of his life, death, burial, and resurrection. A thing he said we have coming as well. Paul said the same before he asked about Death's sting. These are metaphors, the final actuality of which I have not yet experienced. I'll let you know how it goes. But for now I try to identify the ways my fear of Z, of literal and figurative deaths, makes me like one panicking as he drives down the road because he doesn't know what he's seeing—hasn't come to embrace the way of things.

As I get older, incrementally calmer and less concerned with cheating the inevitability of pain and death, I am more able to live. And to Love. Even Jesus didn't get out of death (even if for just three days), so perhaps it's more blessed for me to put most of my energies where he did: mostly into others. This may be the difference between living and merely surviving. Death comes to both pathways, for all of us, but perhaps only one is a story worth telling.

We live in the unending cycles of joy and sorrow, of work and rest, of laughter and weeping, of faith and doubt, of living and dying. This is human life. Fighting against this only makes me miserable. I had this backward for years. I am able to look back to see I've benefited from every single thing that's ever happened to me when I chose to benefit from it. You could say the same.

Our choice to live deciduously is a way of embracing the cycles and seasons, the warm and the cold, the light and the dark, as necessary components of one reality. To live trying to cling to one and avoid the other is a recipe for an anxious, desperate existence. And when I feel this anxious desperation I tend to stop living, cease Loving, and begin trying to make you a pharmacy for my unease. This using each other is, in my experience, the sting and the victory of Death.

Admit it: You have some things going well in your life. But the leaves will someday fall off of it. This is nothing to become anxious or fretful or clingy about. That's just how it goes. Enjoy it. You have some things that have gone to hell in a handbag. Someday those seemingly dead branches will look like life again. It may be a *long* winter. But it's still a season. Those branches will sprout again. You can't escape it. And upsetting yourself solves nothing, so don't forget to do something beyond getting upset. Learn from it. When spring arrives you might be able, from the depths of experience rather than from a book or a sermon, to educate others who think leafless trees are dead trees.

As you look back on things you've suffered, even if you caused this suffering, don't judge it or sweep it under the rug. To deny it is only to lie, which we're trying to move past. See it all, naked and undressed by shame or moralizing, without blame or regret. It's all part of what got you and me to here. And others stand before you and me, friends and family and fellow citizens, with their many hardships and pains too. All of us with our tree rings, the joys and sorrows we've caused and experienced at different and synchronized periods. We accept it, because it's accepted. We hold it in Grace and in Compassion, and we release our fear that whatever difficulty lands on us—or already has— will be the end of us because, well, this ain't our first winter. We know better.

This will be you and me living in the cyclicality of resurrection. And because it's such an inspired way of being in this world, it will also be one of your greatest acts of self-calibrated Love for others.

*On no subject are our ideas more warped and pitiable
than on death. . . . Let children walk with Nature,
let them see the beautiful blendings and communions of death
and life, their joyous inseparable unity, as taught in woods
and meadows, plains and mountains and streams of our
blessed star, and they will learn that death is stingless indeed,
and as beautiful as life, and that the grave has no victory,
for it never fights. All is divine harmony.*
—John Muir

29

Behold, I make
all things nude

THERE IS AN ANCIENT TRADITION of contemplating the beaten
and then crucified body of Christ. And then to consider the
apparent scarring even his resurrected body maintained. For
some it stirs them to guilt, and then in that guilt they behave
themselves for a few days. For far more people it reminds them
of what self-sacrificial Love looks like, what *Ahava* does when
it gives itself to others even at its own expense. It is the locus of
their devotion and gratefulness.

> *See from His head, His hands, His feet,*
> *Sorrow and love flow mingled down!*
> *Did e'er such love and sorrow meet,*
> *Or thorns compose so rich a crown?*
> —Isaac Watts,
> "When I Survey the Wondrous Cross"

But regardless of the motivation to meditate on the wounded Christ, there's one detail about his body that may feel a little strange to fixate on.

Yes, there's the blood.

The nail-scarred hands.

Nail-scarred feet.

Spear-pierced side.

Thorn-stabbed head.

Yes, yes, of course.

But then there's the fact that he was completely naked.

People were crucified naked. Despite Christian art to the contrary, Jesus almost certainly bore sin bare. When he died he was taken down from the cross and was wrapped up in grave clothes and placed in what would by Sunday prove to be a borrowed tomb. The Gospel of John tells us it was a tomb in or adjacent to a garden. Jesus went into it wrapped up like a mummy and the door was sealed.

A seed falling and planted in the dirt. Winter. Dusk.

The following Sunday morning, Jesus wasn't where they put him. The disciples went to confirm the rumor and were devastated to find that the body of their Lord, and the place they would have commemorated him, had been taken from them. Mary Magdalene hung back near the tomb as the men went away drawing up a silly fix to the problem, as men are prone to do.

Suddenly Mary was speaking to a man she didn't immediately recognize. John said she assumed she was speaking to the keeper of the garden.

It would be a few beats until she realized she was speaking

to the very much alive and not dead Jesus of Nazareth. She went from this conversation to tell the others this amazing news, becoming the world's first evangelist of the Resurrected One. Strange how the church has historically been so resistant about women preaching. They started it.

But the detail we often overlook as we talk about the empty tomb is that it wasn't exactly empty. We aren't celebrating an empty tomb technically. When the men who arrived later looked inside, they found grave clothes.

Clothes. Folded neatly according to the narrative. Jesus, the consummate guest.

This unabashedly puts in our minds a nude Jesus exiting the grave if we're paying attention. As one rarely paying full attention to anything, I didn't see any of this until it was pointed out to me. Even John saying, "Mary thought she was speaking to the gardener," which seems a little on the nose to me now, had to be highlighted. Which is important because I was missing more than a mere detail. John, I think, is waving his hands so people like me can understand the fuller beauty of the scene:

A naked Gardener is raised to life in a garden at the end of a book that begins with the same three words as the opening lines of the book of Genesis that features naked gardeners in a Garden: "In the beginning."

Christ has been raised from the dead, the firstfruits of those
who have fallen asleep. For as by a man came death,
by a man has come also the resurrection of the dead.
For as in Adam all die, so also in Christ shall all be made alive. . . .
Thus it is written, "The first man Adam became a living being";
the last Adam became a life-giving spirit.
—Paul, 1 Corinthians 15:20–22, 45

The resurrection, as I hope has become clear, isn't just an assurance of the continuation of life. In that the resurrection of Jesus was like this, naked and vulnerable, harkening back to the original story of unobstructed living connection in the Garden, we seem guided to learn to resurrect now. Like all Kingdom things, it's available wherever we find ourselves. Buried in the field. Lost in our own house. Not so much "there!" or "there!" but within us, waiting to be brought out of the corners of us, uncovered and shameless.

What point is there to any of this if resurrection can only resuscitate corpses but not what's already lifeless in me—dead between you and me—right now? Sure, I have hope about what happens when my biology gives out. As I have trusted God with being born and where that has led, I can trust God with dying and what follows that too. But you and I miss the beauty and the power of resurrection if we keep thinking of it as only getting to live forever. The beauty of death giving way to life now, even as we breathe and walk on this earth. Too often we turn the tradition of following Love himself, the self-sacrificing one, into self-interest and self-preservation. It becomes yet another nervous focus on myself, with a cross painted on it.

O loving wisdom of our God!
When all was sin and shame,
A second Adam to the fight
And to the rescue came.
—John Henry Newman,
"Praise to the Holiest in the Height"

Resurrection is one of quite a few things I neither know about, nor have any firsthand experience with. But it is also one of a few things I can say with confidence are worth opening myself to and being transformed by. In this latter category, resurrection is an invitation to begin living unpretentiously, honestly, and vulnerably, now. Your stomach will knot when you hear this invitation clearly, in a given moment, because Christ is saying far more than we're initially comfortable with when he says, "Follow me." He wasn't inviting us to church, after all. Christ is inviting us back out of a fetid grave into light, with no coverings and no fear and nothing between us. I think we resist resurrection's terms for much the same reason we have that naked-in-school dream: fear of being found out. Being seen and known, as well as truly knowing, are truly troubling when life has been up to that point a safely performed show. But we aren't practicing very well for eternity if we learn a bunch of Bible trivia while keeping our cautious, defensive pants on. However terrifying and hazardous it feels, our forgiveness of ourselves and others, our mutual validation, our suspended criticisms, our respecting the other enough to put away hierarchy and sham, our rewarding one's honesty over one's ideological alignment, our fighting every day to celebrate our oneness in the face of our culture's insistence on separateness—all this is the revealing, vulnerable, apocalyptic work of Love.

And it's what you and I, and the Spirit who made us, want more than anything.

It is better to live naked in truth than clothed in fantasy.
—Brennan Manning

30

→

Look out below

PONTIUS PILATE COULDN'T UNDERSTAND what the big deal was. The crowd was worked up to a lather about this Jesus fella from Nazareth and him being guilty of some crime or another. Lord have mercy, there were always fires to put out in this part of the Roman Empire.

Pilate had just volleyed a few times with this Jesus in an inner room, finding himself confounded by a discussion about what's true. "What is truth?" asked the man who did business like this in back rooms, where his incompetence might not be seen or counted against his aspirations for Caesar's right hand, and maybe even someday his throne.

"I've interviewed him." Pilate had come back out into the light of day to address the angry assembly. "I don't see that he's guilty of anything more than being related to you all."

"He claimed to be king!" yelled one.

"He threatened to destroy our temple," said another.

"He thinks he's God. But we lack the sovereignty to execute him for it!" It was a dog pile now.

Pontius rubbed his head, wishing Passover would pass over. It was customary to release a prisoner to the Jews every spring. To *let one of their people go.* The irony of Pontius, a powerful leader whose name loosely translates as "Sea," allowing the Exodus of a Hebrew was probably not lost on many in the crowd.

"This year for release, how about I release to you this King of you Jews." He was trying to put out a fire with sarcasm now. He must not have been married for very long at this point to still be using this tactic.

"No!" they screamed. "Not him. Give us Barabbas!"

Barabbas is labeled here in the story as a thief. But his brand of thievery was different from the guy who busts your window to take your car stereo. Barabbas was an insurrectionist. A Robin Hood type, who led brigands who may or may not have been merry to take from those who had and redistribute it to those who didn't. Barabbas was a revolutionary hoping for an uprising. He was perhaps what many today would even call a terrorist.

Barabbas, whose surname is Aramaic and literally means "son of a father," would have had a following. Supporters. Teens would have worn Barabbas T-shirts. Parents would have been torn over whether a guy like Barabbas was of God, or of something else. Barabbas had a vision. A call to arms to anyone faithful enough to respond. Doubtless he spoke powerful words about what it would require to take the world back from the corrupted powers and set it all right. To return Israel to her glory days, whenever that was. There was a way things ought to be. And any means to get there were justified by that Glorious End. Murder, upheaval, reversal of power. To God be the glory. He'd gotten himself, and no doubt a few of his captains, arrested for gaining momentum.

Some ancient manuscripts of this passage show Barabbas's first name was Jesus. It is thought by some that copyists, who wanted to honor God and the Scripture, took Barabbas's first name out years after the Gospels were written so that there wouldn't be confusion. Pilate even refers to Jesus as "Jesus who is called Christ," which is a strange thing to clarify unless clarification needed to be made.

The scene is rather uncomfortable if you allow it to be as uncomfortable as it seems intended to be: There are two Jesuses, each with a vision and a kingdom and a power and a glory, one on each side of Pilate for faithful folks to choose between.

"Do you Jews want me to pardon Jesus Barabbas?" Pontius Pilate was asking. "Do you want the revolutionary who seeks to change things with violence and domination? The one who wants to change how people are and how systems work and what people value by using the very tactics of the government that incarcerated him? You want the one with the strategy that appeals to your delusions of power, and the chops to garner a following . . ."

Or . . .

"Do you want this other Jesus? A so-called revolutionary, with a vision, yes, but who goes about things differently, does he not? He speaks of a Kingdom superseding Caesar's while he plays with children, treats women like humans, touches rejects, surrounds himself with bad résumés, and washes the feet of people too stupid to decipher the gesture. One who forgives to the point of irresponsibility and who says the trajectory of true Compassion is the ability to Love even your enemy."

"Do you all want Jesus the son of a father, or Jesus the Son of the Father?"

"Give us our Jesus Barabbas. We want to win!"

So the guards took Jesus who was called Christ, beat him

within an inch of his life, and then took that last inch as well. Barabbas went home and got a shower, but never did feel like he could get clean of it all, because you can only pretend not to recognize *Ahava* when confronted with it.

And before I start shaking my head at how all of this unfolded, I should probably admit to myself that I often ask for Jesus Barabbas. It's hard to blame the people back then. They were really looking for a powerful figure to follow, one who could turn things around. One who would overthrow corrupt power and give folks their lives back. Jesus went to Jerusalem to die; what lasting good could underthrowing the powers that be possibly accomplish? He did not have a strong campaign on the face of it. Who in their right mind votes for the one promising to self-terminate?

The people wanted something they thought would work. Like I do. Like you do. "Give us someone great! We want to be part of something great! This Jesus is the wrong direction if we're ever going to have lives worth living."

I'm sure I would have been right there chanting Barabbas's name with them. And not as one of a hissing, bloodthirsty crowd in some Jesus movie. I probably would have had a good reason. I would have probably been there because I am often tempted to believe that if life is going to change—if my world, my city, my culture, my marriage, my kids, my schools, are going to make it all the way through—then we need someone who can overpower that which works against it. To bring in some muscle to save it. How else will I know we succeeded but for the fact that our guy doesn't die and their guys do? I would have been there chanting for the Jesus who could secure a win for my team.

I find the more unaddressed my interior, the more evasive I am about the light of Truth, the more I resist honesty, the more I believe in what's little more than childish, animal kingdom power. If the inside world remains unconquered, then the whole expanse of the exterior universe goes in the crosshairs. This may be why people most at peace with their interior don't want to be in charge of much. Whenever I've not faced my inner world, I'll start trying to futz with yours. Every time.

When Jesus got into the city earlier that week, he all but set the scene up for his disciples:

"I tell you honestly, unless a seed falls into the earth and dies, it remains just that, a seed. But if it allows itself to die, it bears much fruit. Whoever prioritizes the preserving of his own life ends up losing it, and whoever resists this impulse will find themselves living an eternal quality of life now and forever. If anyone wants to serve my interests, he must follow me on this path. So that wherever I am, others will see my servants are there too."

It's almost too risky to adopt. It reads wonderfully on Sunday morning, but in the real day-to-day life, this is insanity. Especially when it matters most. Why would I rationally choose your interests over mine? Why would I spend my life's energies calibrating myself to give your interest priority? Why would I choose to throw the game for the opponent? Especially if that opponent seems wrong/evil/bad/dumb?

Nice sermon, Pastor, but what about ISIS and my ex-husband?

We've been trying for millennia to figure out how to take up a cross *and* also snag a win. How we might both gain our souls *and* the world. How we put off the old self, as Paul put it, while also fighting tooth and nail to be the fittest, as Darwin framed. Give me the choice not to lose and I'll take it. Who would blame me?

And yet, over generations, we sense there's a better story than what makes us chant Barabbas's name. Something truer to our nature, lying beneath our anxieties and vigilances. A better story that doesn't simply praise losing, but praises Christ and isn't afraid to lose if that's the best way for Christ's self-sacrificing Love to mend what's broken. Faith in resurrection, the embrace of truth in exchange for the releasing of the fear of deaths.

How do we *know* it's the better story? One clue to me is that you have never been to the Church of Barabbas. That movement didn't take. Despite it being tried every couple of generations, those roots never got into the bedrock of the deepest human story. Asking for Barabbas seems more assured, more intelligent when life shows up in all its intensity. You may never feel more foolish than when in an argument, or when faced with decisions that might make or break your company, you realize you've signed on to follow the Prince of Peace while the moment seems to demand a ruthless swordsman. Yet in our depths, if we'll lean over the rim of that well and listen, it's the way of *that Jesus* that stirs us, promises real healing, and delivers. Jesus Barabbas, to the surprise of anyone who believes in a commonsense kind of power, was a nonstarter. What *did* start, slow and problematic in every age, was the one who looked like weak, suicidal idealism dressed up in the nonsense of the spiritually naive: Love. Hope. Forgiveness. Others-centering. The one who chose others over self made it all the way through. Look around at life and our world, and hear Pilate asking which Jesus we want. Which Jesus can walk us all the way through. It's a choice we must make every day.

It's the heart of *Ahava*, our true self, which responds to Christ's crazy, unabated idea. Even as our worried minds call all this unrealistic, we hear it, we read it, we see glimpses of it at work or in traffic or at college, we feel the whisper of the cosmos calling to us to take note, and embers within us pop back into flame. *Dare to Love like Christ, to live as one unafraid of the truth or of death or of anything. Dare to even now, in this moment.* We will continue to resist this whisper from time to time, bombing our enemies and yelling at our family members and cobbling an identity out of outperforming our neighbors and shunning our vulnerability even as we feel hollow inside. Even the church unwittingly chants the name of Jesus Barabbas when things get hard. We're all capable of returning to survival of the fittest, a life given its dimension by little more than avoiding loss. But like a rubber band snapping back, like a Word that cannot return void, a better story calls us home with a knowing smile. And for those with eyes to see, with ears to hear, Christ's way reveals itself to be all we ever wanted. I really don't think I've overstated that: we all want to be what we are—*Ahava*—and the Christ shows us again and again what it looks like.

It should be pointed out that Jesus didn't stop at the seed and the dying and losing thing. He added a bit about following him. Which we can reasonably assume means right into the maw of death, into forgiving those responsible for it, and out the other side, prepared to watch the world be recalibrated by our unfathomably powerful Love. By our growing tolerance for the strangling pain our fight-or-flee programming was designed to avoid. He didn't invite his students to merely agree. We're supposed to go and do this, work it all out in the real world.

Though I am incrementally more willing to be one who dies as an act of my own will, I'm a seed with hands too strong for my own good, clutching the vine in desperation, unwilling to be obscured or forgotten, to suffer the loss of too much *me*. I can, though, cheerfully report that I am losing faith in the way of Barabbas, because I've tried to make revolution his way and it's only made me tired. It's only turned out to be ultimately hurtful to others who need my Love, rather than my control. The spirit of Barabbas is fruitless. You can't grow trees from a nut too afraid to let go of its branch and die.

Who knew trying not to die would be the thing that got us so grafted to death? Who knew that true strength was the bleeding, weak thing we sent away to the cross in order that we might secure the "win." Most of us can only recognize all of this in hindsight—a fair explanation of how the Scriptures do their inspiring. But spiritual giants from traditions the world over have been saying it for generations, from the margins and in the wild, where we thought losers went, that surrender—not apathy or fatalism, but openhanded surrender—has always been the key

to living our lives to Manufacturer specifications. So, here's to it. Here's to all us nuts having our grip weakened so that we might drop off the branch, so we might see the benefit of a crucified, buried, and resurrected Christ even as those who hang on keep chanting for the other guy. Here's to believing there's more life to be found on the far side of the deaths we're so good at avoiding.

31

Conquered

THE ONE WHO CAME TO GIVE LIFE, buckets of it, was now stapled naked and dead on a criminal's execution stake. The One in whom the hopes of human salvation were hung now hung slack, dripping. Imagine telling aliens this was our world's dominant religion's symbol of hope. We really do wear crosses around our necks to enhance our appearance. Strange. How could a species so easily persuaded that the only way forward is putting others in the very position Jesus was in on that cross explain to another species that this scene was the epitome of Good?

A man stopped me after a sermon one Sunday, a couple of weeks before Easter, to tell me I had spoken well and that he was thankful.

"Great sermon, Steve, those were good words. Thank you." He shook my hand with enough squeeze in it to communicate his idea of strength. "All of that *take up your cross, love your enemy stuff, self-sacrifice stuff* sounds great in here. It really does. But you know, at the end of the day, in the real world, my trust is in our tanks and my AR-15."

When the centurion, who stood there in front of Jesus,
saw how he died, he said,
"Surely this man was the Son of God!"
—Mark 15:39 NIV

It's likely this centurion, a trained killer and leader of a hundred of Rome's finest, had been in charge of everything that happened to Jesus after Pilate sentenced him. He'd overseen Jesus being whipped to shreds. He'd observed him beaten and mocked. He'd seen the insults hurled at him from his own people. Like he had countless times before with so many other accused, the centurion had overseen this Jesus being tacked up on a tree so the public could see his body and his reputation die.

But what he hadn't seen in this teacher's last words and actions is probably what caught his attention. Unlike so many criminals executed before, he never saw this Jesus become ugly or disparaging. Not one time did he blame anyone. He didn't spit back, swing, argue, or threaten. He wept and groaned, but without venom.

And honest to God, the man even prayed for the forgiveness of those involved in his crucifixion, calling them ignorant rather than evil.

The centurion had never been prayed for by one he was killing. It was as though this man from Nazareth had kept himself untouched from the very hate that was murdering him. It was a strength rooted in a very different soil than he himself, a conquering Roman, had been planted in.

Yes, the man still died. It wasn't as though subverting retaliation and the instinct for violence was a "get out of death" card.

But long before the Christian tradition teaches that the Holy Ghost came upon the first disciples, this centurion was haunted.

"Son of God" was a title already in use. The known world applied it to Caesar. We can find the phrase on coins and columns from Roman antiquity. Like so many despots before and after, Caesar's power came largely from his being perceived as the savior of mankind, the absolute principal of the civilized world. Caesar was the head of the empire—the king of the kingdom of peace, according to the propaganda. Anyone who disagreed was subject to slaughter in the name of this peace. It's as inspired as when you and I yell at our children to stop screaming. The centurion protected and expanded the reign of the son of god, to death.

Stunned into spontaneous confession, he looked at this Nazarene bleeding out on a cross, mocked with a sarcastic sign about his supposed kingship mounted over his crimson head, and perhaps for the first time in his life saw something more powerful than "power." We can't know what happened next for the centurion. Perhaps that doesn't matter. Perhaps seeing a slight shift from one trained under the ideology of *Pax Romana*—peace at gunpoint, harmony created by aggressive intolerance to anything outside the pattern of domination and control—is enough. When someone who has achieved our fundamental understanding of power comes to deem Jesus's self-sacrifice as worthy of awe, maybe that's enough story for us to benefit from forever.

Compassion trumped the vicious brutality required of a person to nail Jesus to a tree. And a man trained in simplistic definitions of victory was transformed by it.

Theological explanations aside, the murder of Jesus wasn't

fair or right. Outside of the faith tradition, we'd say the killing of Jesus could and should have been avoided. But it happened, and it happened in such a way that it cancelled out sin and brutality rather than escalating it. What was arguably fair—a scenario where those responsible for Jesus's death, and those responsible for the way of death, were murdered rather than Jesus—was suspended for what was Good—the giving of the self so that Love, Grace, Compassion, Forgiveness, and Faithfulness might never be confused with something merely theoretical again. Thank God we never had to name it Fair Friday.

Men and women of incredible Love, confidence, and self-control, not reacting to the evil of their circumstances but somehow absorbing it, transforming it, show us in our own time some of what stunned the centurion. Refusing to let the craziness spiral on for even a moment more, cutting off the volleying darkness of revenge and cruelty and condescension because they realize good can only come when one chooses not so much to win but to forgive—this is a taste of Christ's Way. These folks who astonish us by circumventing something like Newton's third law by not pushing back with the same force, the same level of consciousness, aimed at them. They respond under a different Law, and the energy of harm is absorbed. It can't always be done. And sometimes it can be done and isn't. Alas, even this inconstancy is absorbed. We're invited to gather these sorts of folk together with the rest of us. Ideally, we can call it a church. Those who show us the power of such Love, such ability to absorb rather than reflect evil back; Christ lives the loudest through such people. Deep down, you and I *are* all such people.

And we are forgiven and embraced even when we refuse to be such people, forget we are such people, or can't find a way to remain such people.

> *You have heard people say, "An eye for an eye and*
> *a tooth for a tooth." But I tell you, "Don't get into tug-o-wars*
> *with those who are evil. Instead, if anyone slaps you*
> *on the right cheek, turn to him the left also."*
> —Jesus, Matthew 5:38–39, my rendering

The King absorbed evil on Good Friday like even the dimmest candle chews up the darkness in a room. Because of this, the world would be gradually, over decades and centuries, grabbed by the collar and shaken gently into various stages of wakefulness. And here we are, generations later, staring at a cross just as bewildered and inspired as the centurion who first recognized that "Son of God" might have been misattributed to one who merely avoided losing.

Wait a minute.

Is this how the world is saved?

By overcoming evil with Love rather than with more evil?

By forgiving and considering rather than justifying any means required to win?

By absorbing a wrong rather than retaliating against it?

By behaving not as a nation that can do little more than defend itself from outsiders and troublesome insiders, but as a family member growing in awareness that everyone—everyone!—is invited to the reunion?

In Christ all the fullness of God was pleased to dwell,
and through Christ to reconcile to himself everything,
whether things on earth or things in heaven,
making peace for everything by the blood of his cross.
—Colossians 1:19–20, my rendering

Consequences for selfish, harmful behaviors still happen. Hurtful people are still confronted, apprehended, and insulated so that their uncalibrated selfishness can't easily be inflicted on others. Lines are sometimes unavoidably drawn between this one and that one so that the healing we're trying to get to can even begin to happen. You don't put dangerous dogs with the others, no matter how big a dog lover you are. But if you're a dog lover, you know that with Compassion and care that dog will probably be a beloved part of the pack again someday.

Paul pled with his early church, "Don't return evil for evil, but instead overcome evil with good." The man seemed to think *good* has an overcoming power. If this sounds hard, like it would require some assistance, then I am communicating effectively. The word *excruciating* is a Latin term that means "of the cross." They had to invent a new word for the kind of pain one endures when they believe in the Love required to make a centurion say, "Hang on just a minute. I gotta rethink everything." Anybody can become the smell of the crap being thrown at them. It takes real strength, real inspiration, to have it thrown at you and end up smelling like Christ anyway. Don't take my word for it. Take it up with the centurion.

I should add something here. People must never misunderstand faith as letting abusive people abuse you. This isn't what

"self-sacrificial" is getting at. "It's her cross to bear" is one abomi-
nable rendition of this misunderstanding I've heard recently. A
woman was being abused by a husband who repeatedly threw
two-hundred-pound tantrums at her when things didn't go his
way. A pastor looked her in her swollen eyes and told her to
forgive and serve the animal. "It was God's will," he said, going
afterward to his own home and she to hers. If God, who is
Love, who is delicate, gentle Compassion, is pleased by our being abused, then we should feel at liberty to switch religions.
I'll repeat it for those among us most wounded by the untuned
self-interest of others: sometimes the power of Love demands
we get distance between us and those who'd do us or our loved
ones harm, making as sure as possible they cannot harm anyone else. In the name of Love, get away from the evil happening
and as compassionately as possible, neutralize the foolishness of
fools. This isn't weakness. It's intelligence. It's appropriately self-
interested, which, as we have seen, is good and necessary and
wholly spiritual.

But we don't have to meet selfishness and evil on its terms.
The invitation and challenge in our getting our distance and
making sure someone's evil is brought to justice can now be done
from a power greater than the spirit of a threatened Caesar, a
maneuvering Pilate, a vengeful Barabbas. Now we are awakened
to a Love that refuses to become the shadow that fell on us, but
instead seeks to bring Light. Light kills darkness naturally. Mold
withers in the sun. Do not take revenge, as Paul said. Let God do
that. It's better. Harder oftentimes, but better. I don't know how
this works scientifically so I don't offer a formula: but the same
Spirit that astounded the centurion is available to all of us who

have been crucified, and all of us who have swung the hammer as well.

The cross perhaps confronts us about the very hardest part about being a human being stuck living with other human beings. But it's far harder, far more miserable to maintain citizenship in the Empire of the Tick. That's a world maintained by nervously acquiring and defending, taking and retaking in the name of self. It's a nervous place with wide gates that everyone's rushing. To live apart from our essential Loving nature is low resistance but even lower joy. However unintuitive, it's more blessed to give—not just our money, for crying out loud, but *everything we are!*—than to receive. It's not easy living in tune with what we are. Christ assured us it wouldn't be, for whatever that reminder may be worth. Christ, remember, got it right and was killed. And yet Christ lives again, still inviting us with a "Follow me," his beckoning hand scarred. You and I might need a few decades to mean it when we answer *yes*.

Let us entertain that we are being offered a place in the rescue of not just some folks but all of them, and of everything. It is all Loved, because it all comes from Love. You. Me. Victims. Agents. Right people. Wrong people. Us. Them. All of it. So we're part of something big, and something with as many of us in view as are willing to say yes.

So let us say yes. Every day. Let us have our simplistic, fear-born notions about this God—this infinite Love—dismantled. Let *us* be dismantled. Let us find our growing in kindness enough religion for a lifetime, and let's save much kindness for ourselves. Let us start tearing holes in the roof if we find the traditional church too full of people on their own two feet for us to fit through the door. Let us not carry shame and fear one more day. Neither let us contribute to others carrying theirs. Let us know and believe the crazy idea that it's as we are poured out that we are full. Let us find ourselves awakened and saying to each other, somewhat surprised and confused, "Oh yeah! *This* is the Son of God. *This* is Love. *This* is everything."

And then let us get going, and be this too. After all, we most truly are.

NOTES

Hat tips

I OWE A TREMENDOUS THANK-YOU to countless folks with whom I've exchanged ideas, debated, laughed, and cried. All that birthed the thoughts in this book. These dear people have, over the years, helped me see that something beautiful happens when Love and unassailable inclusion intersect. To name you is a whole other book! Thank you all.

Thank you, Jana Burson, my wonderful agent, who gushed praise on an early draft of this book. I sat in my son's carpool line listening to you carry on about my writing, wondering if you'd called the wrong client. Your encouragement and savvy then and now has been formative. Thank you to the whole team at Worthy Publishing. You've been so encouraging, patient, and excited about *Experiments in Honesty* from the first day you held unedited pages in your hands. Thank you, Kyle, for helping get those pages edited. Thank you, Jeana, for reminding me that if I'm not helping people feel something, I'm not helping people. Thank you, Caroline, Nicole, and Leeanna, for your enthusiasm and guidance in getting my words into more hands. Also Bart and the whole design team for making the book beautiful inside and out.

The people at my church, Crosspointe in Cary, have been nothing but encouraging and supportive. Thank you all for cheering me on, giving me ideas, and helping me believe this was worth seeing through to the end. Thanks, Ben, for helping with my web stuff. Thanks, Janet, for helping me know what to do with my drawings. Thanks, Kris, for helping with the English language in general. And Don, thanks for helping to put me in front of so many thousands of people over the years to hone my craft. Sushi Tuesday? To all of you, I've never wondered if you were behind me on this.

Thank you, Jonathan and Stephen, for reading early manuscripts and highlighting where I maybe sounded more like someone else than myself. In the midst of the busy, often weird work we do, thank you for celebrating and prioritizing my efforts in publishing *Experiments*. For letting me bounce these words off of you here and there, so that they never got too theoretical. For being dear friends who made me feel like a dear friend. Thank you, TJ, for long sacred talks that kept front of mind that the Story is far greater than how we typically frame it. That it's so good it scares us. And to all the leadership at Crosspointe, thanks for never framing the energy I've given to this writing as a debit on my day job. That's a testament to your faith, and to your love for me. Thank you. You all get a 15 percent discount on this book.

And thank you, Kristi, my dear wife, for knowing how wide the gap is between what I'd like to be and who I actually am, and for loving me anyway. I happen to know better than anyone how hard that is to do. You have been so encouraging that you've even been that wonderful kind of frustrated with me when I've needed it. This went from a "Hey, wouldn't it be cool . . ." to a published reality because you pushed and reminded and encouraged. You'll never receive proper credit, but you deserve it. Thank you for letting me be at your side. You get 1 (one) free copy. Signed, even.

Scriptural references

Chapter 1

Jesus in the boat with the apostles, Luke 5:1–11 and Mark 1:16–18,
my rendering

Peter on the mountain with Jesus, Matthew 17:1–8, my rendering

Peter sending children away from Jesus, Luke 18:15–17

Peter sending hungry people away, Matthew 14:13–21

Peter rebuking Jesus about Jesus's death, Matthew 16:21–24

Peter slicing the soldier's ear, Matthew 26:50–55

Jesus telling about Peter's denials, Mark 14:27–30, my rendering

Peter declaring Jesus is the Christ, Matthew 16:13–17 (v. 16)

Fear of the Lord is the beginning of wisdom, Proverbs 1:7, 9:10,
Psalm 111:10, my rendering

"The God Who Sees," Genesis 16:13–14, my rendering

How God sees versus how people see, 1 Samuel 16:7, my rendering

Chapter 2

Jesus telling Peter he would build his church on him, the rock,
Matthew 16:18

Chapter 3

The Samaritan woman at the well, John 4:1–42, my rendering

Jesus is the way, the truth, and the life, John 14:6

Adam and Eve, Genesis 2–3

"All have sinned . . . ," Romans 3:23

Pontius Pilate asking Jesus questions, John 18:38

Chapter 5

Paul's "Fruit of the Spirit," Galatians 5:22–23

"Let thieves no longer steal . . . ," Ephesians 4:28, my rendering

Chapter 6

"Do this in remembrance of me," Luke 22:19, my rendering

"I came that they may have life, and have it abundantly," Jesus,
John 10:10

"God is love," 1 John 4:8, 4:16

"You love all the things that are," Wisdom of Solomon 11:24
(Apocrypha)

Chapter 7

"No one has ever seen God," John 1:18 , 1 John 4:12, 1 John 4:20,
1 Timothy 1:17, and 1 Timothy 6:16

Unapproachable Light, 1 Timothy 6:14–16

God is fire, Exodus 19:18 and Hebrews 12:29

God is (or causes) smoke, Exodus 19:18 and Isaiah 6:4

God has no form, Deuteronomy 4:15

Fall of man, Genesis 3:1–13

Paul's being warring with his spirit, Romans 7:14–20

Chapter 9

"Do this in remembrance of me," Luke 22:19

"Which is the great commandment . . . ," Matthew 22:36–40

"Whatever you wish that others would do to you . . . ," Matthew
7:12

"If you really fulfill the royal law according to the Scripture . . . ,"
James 2:8

"You shall love your neighbor as yourself . . . ," Romans 13:9–10

"It's more blessed to give than to receive," from Acts 20:35

Chapter 10

Moses asks to see God, Exodus 33:18–20

"The Lord is Compassionate," Exodus 34:6, my rendering

"The least of the these," Matthew 25:40

"Love your enemy," Matthew 5:43–48, my rendering

Chapter 11

God's Word doesn't return void, Isaiah 55:11

"Which commandment is the most important of all?" Mark 12:28–34,
    my rendering

Paul taught us to observe other traditions, Acts 17:16–34 and
    1 Corinthians 3:21–23

Different traditions' Golden Rule, www.scarboromissions.ca/golden-rule

"Follow me," Matthew 4:19

Chapter 12

Jesus called them hypocrites, Matthew 23:13, 15

Chapter 13

"Jesus, teach us to pray," Luke 11:1–13, my rendering

God is "slow to anger," Exodus 34:6; Numbers 14:18; Psalm 86:15; and
    Jonah 4:2

"If you've seen me you've seen the Father," John 14:9, my rendering

Christ is the "exact imprint" of God, Hebrews 1:3

Paul's "Fruit of the Spirit," Galatians 5:22–23

Chapter 14

Jesus warns against throwing pearls before swine, Matthew 7:6

Chapter 15

Sermon on the Mount, Matthew 5–7

"Crowds," Matthew 5:1

"Happy are . . ." Beatitudes, Matthew 5:1–12, my rendering

"You are the salt . . . ," Matthew 5:13–16, my rendering

Moses talk bad, Exodus 4:10–11

Gideon the wimp, Judges 6:15

Jeremiah too young, Jeremiah 1:1–6

Paul wrote better than he looked, 2 Corinthians 10:10

Paul terrorized the church, Acts 9:1–2

End of Jesus's public ministry, Matthew 28:16–20, my rendering

Chapter 16

The Kingdom is in our midst, Luke 17:21

Chapter 17

Flesh versus Spirit, Galatians 5:17

"Flesh" understood as "Ego," Richard Rohr, *Immortal Diamond: The Search for Our True Self* (San Francisco: Jossey-Bass, 2013)

Paul to Galatian family, Galatians 5:13–14, my rendering

Chapter 19

Anointing Jesus with perfume, Matthew 26:6–13, Mark 14:3–9, Luke 7:36–50, John 12:1–8, my rendering

Chapter 20

Kingdom belongs to children, Matthew 19:14

Jesus's healing loogie, Mark 8:22–25, my rendering

Chapter 21

John the Baptist thrown in jail, Luke 3:18–20

Jesus begins his ministry when John is imprisoned, Mark 1:14–15

"To Life!" is "L'Chaim!"

Carry one another's loads, Galatians 6:2

Chapter 22
The Lord's Prayer, Matthew 6:9–13, my rendering

Chapter 23
Jesus heals and forgives the paralytic on a mat, Mark 2:1–12, my rendering

Chapter 25
The truth sets us free, John 8:32

Chapter 26
"Don't worry," Matthew 6:25, my rendering
"Don't worry like the Gentiles do," Matthew 6:32, my rendering
"Seek first God's Kingdom," Matthew 6:33, my rendering
"Do not judge . . . ," Matthew 7:1–5, my rendering
"Not my will but yours," Luke 22:42, my rendering

Chapter 27
Every tribe, every language, every nation, Revelation 7:9

Chapter 28
"Where, O Death, is your sting?" 1 Corinthians 15:55, my rendering
"Unless a seed dies . . . ," John 12:24

Chapter 29
Jesus's tomb in a garden, John 19:41
"Empty" tomb and Jesus the Gardener, John 20:1–16, my rendering
The Kingdom isn't so much "there" or "there," Luke 17:21

Chapter 30
Jesus before Pilate, "Give us Barabbas," Matthew 27:11–26, Mark 15:1–15, Luke 23:1–25, John 18:28–40, my rendering

Barabbas's name was Jesus, Craig A. Evans, *Matthew, New Cambridge Bible Commentary* (Cambridge University Press, 2012), 453

"Unless a seed dies . . . ," John 12:24–26, my rendering

"Put off the old self," Ephesians 4:22–24

Chapter 31

"Never repay evil for evil . . . ," Romans 12:17–18, my rendering

Christ assured us this wouldn't be easy, John 16:33

"All of it," Colossians 1:20